Touching God :
52 Guidelines for Personal Prayer

Touching God

52 Guidelines for Personal Prayer

Harold J. Sala, Ph.D.

CHRISTIAN PUBLICATIONS, INC.
CAMP HILL, PENNSYLVANIA

Christian Publications, Inc.
3825 Hartzdale Drive, Camp Hill, PA 17011
www.cpi-horizon.com
www.christianpublications.com

Touching God: 52 Guidelines for Personal Prayer
ISBN: 0-87509-862-2
LOC Catalog Card Number: 99-080102

00 01 02 03 04   5 4 3 2 1

Affectionately dedicated to

Armin Gesswein,

the father of the modern prayer movement.

But more than that,
I will always remember him
as a personal mentor,
Dad-in-the-Lord
and dear friend
whose life has embodied prayer.

Contents

Foreword ix

Preface. xi

Day 1 Find Out about Prayer. 1

Day 2 Lord, Teach Us to Pray 5

Day 3 Our Father. 9

Day 4 Where Is God's Heaven?. 13

Day 5 Let Your Kingdom Come 17

Day 6 Thine Is the Kingdom 21

Day 7 Getting Things Done through Prayer 25

Day 8 Prayer Is a Dialogue 29

Day 9 Conversational Prayer 33

Day 10 Because You Are Important 37

Day 11 The Privileges of the Son 41

Day 12 In the Presence of the Father 45

Day 13 Prayer Is Based on a Relationship 49

Day 14 The Prayer Difference 53

Day 15 Programming 57

Day 16 How Long Should You Pray? 61

Day 17 What's on Your Prayer List?. 65

Day 18 When You Pray, Forgive. 69

Day 19 Praying with Thanksgiving 73

Day 20 Answered Prayer—God's Way. 77

Day 21 The Four Laws of Answered Prayer 81

Day 22 Focusing on the Father 85

Day 23 Beyond "God, This . . ." 89

Day 24 Ambrose Whaley's Spiritual Secret 93

Day 25 The Undiscovered Power of Prayer 97

Day 26 My House Will Be Called a House of Prayer . . 101

Day 27 Why Not? 105

Day 28 Praying in the Will of God 109

Day 29 If God Doesn't Answer Prayer 113

Day 30 Prayer in Churches 117

Day 31 Praying for Your Pastor 121

Day 32 Ask Chris Milbrath If Prayer
         Makes a Difference 125

Day 33 The Power of the Bended Knee 129

Day 34 Praying as a Couple 133

Day 35 Prayer Therapy and Marriage 137

Day 36 Pray and Grow Rich 141

Day 37 Having Confidence with God 145

Day 38 Prayer for a Missionary in Trouble 149

Day 39 A Spontaneous Explosion of Prayer 153

Day 40 Rees Howells 157

Day 41 Praying without an Agenda 161

Day 42 One Man's Prayer 165

Day 43 Answers to Prayers We Never Prayed 169

Day 44 How Many Times Must You Ask? 173

Day 45 Going One-on-One with God in Trusting Him . 177

Day 46 Going One-on-One with God in Prayer 181

Day 47 Going One-on-One with God in Faith 185

Day 48 When God's Answer Doesn't
         Match Your Request 189

Day 49 When God Says, "My Grace Is Enough!" . . . 193

Day 50 When the Grass Is Growing on Your Path . . . 197

Day 51 Praying without the Amen 201

Day 52 If You Could Ask One Question 205

Foreword

I have known Harold Sala for a lot of years and have watched his life and ministry unfold like a flower.

In his manifold ministry (radio and television, conferences and many missionary endeavors) with Guidelines, Inc., which he founded and directs, he is a very busy man. He does so many things and does them well.

In reality, however, they all come out of one thing: *prayer*. And let me quickly add *faith*. Prayer without faith is dead, and Dr. Sala always takes his faith along when he prays. He is also a part of our Prayer Fellowship, and when he prays he believes the Lord is hearing and answering. The answers keep coming—large and small—in his personal life and in his many ministries.

He has learned that *everything* in life is made for prayer, and it is inviting and exciting to hear him tell how the Lord is constantly leading with one answer to prayer after another. The answers never cease. And this includes finances. His life story is one of prayer and answered prayer.

So when Harold Sala talks about prayer and answered prayer we listen.

He also has a very large writing ministry, covering almost every facet of the Christian life. In the following chapters he has crafted many vignettes, and they all relate to his own prayer life. This gives them a quality of their own, one which you will enjoy at the same time that you will be inspired in your own life of prayer and answered prayer.

You will find these to be guidelines not only for prayer, but also for living.

Armin Gesswein
Director, Revival Prayer Fellowship, Inc.

Preface

ℛecently a friend of Guidelines called, saying that he was going to speak on the subject of prayer, and he asked if I could send him some of the selections which have been aired on my radio program, "Guidelines for Living." As I began searching, I was amazed at the number of selections—some of which were released several years ago—which contained inspiration and encouragement.

Not only was his heart blessed, but mine was as well as I began to ponder the awesome power of prayer which is often neglected and not practiced. Yes, we believe in the power of prayer, but often it is relegated to the spiritual 911 category (help, God, I'm in big trouble!).

I have prepared this anthology of selections on prayer—some of which have previously been printed in *Today Can Be the Best Day of Your Life* and *365 Guidelines for Living*—to serve as an encouragement for your personal prayer life.

Each one stands alone. You will get the most out of this book by reading one each day and then applying the truths you have learned to your personal life.

Naturally, I would be pleased to hear from you. Please let me know how your prayer life has been enriched and your spiritual roots have gone deeper as your faith has risen higher.

Tennyson was right: "More things are wrought by prayer than this world ever dreamed of."

Yours and His,

Harold J. Sala
Guidelines International Ministries
Box G
Laguna Hills, CA 92654

𝒥IND OUT ABOUT PRAYER

*"But God has surely listened and
heard my voice in prayer." (Psalm 66:19)*

𝒞harles Steinmetz was an electrical genius. He was a gifted scientist and inventor who discovered the principles of direct electrical current. This man took his place in the halls of science alongside Thomas Edison (who invented the incandescent globe), Alexander Bell (who invented the telephone) and Enrico Fermi (who split the atom). He was slight of stature and as the result of a spinal injury stood slightly stooped forward. Toward the end of his life, he was asked what field of scientific research offered the greatest promise in the future. His answer surprised some as he said, "Prayer. Find out about prayer!"

The man who discovered direct electrical current also was interested in spiritual current. "Find out about prayer," he said. When I accidentally touch a live wire, I know it. There is no questioning the fact that I discovered the current! My hair stands on end and I jump.

Does prayer work the same way? When Jesus prayed, the request and the answer seemed to flow along the same lines, the same current. It was not a "leave your request at the door and I'll get back to you as soon as possible" sort of relationship. When Jesus prayed, things happened. That was why the disciples came to Jesus with the request, "Lord, teach us to pray!" (Luke 11:1).

In time, the disciples found out about prayer. They prayed in all kinds of circumstances: in homes where they met for fellowship, in the temple, in prison where they had been thrown for preaching the gospel, in confronting disease and illness. They prayed in almost every conceivable situation, giving us a pattern to follow.

> *Prayer is talking with your Heavenly Father, and the conversation should just flow out of your heart.*

"Find out about prayer," urged Charles Steinmetz.

One way you can find out about prayer is simply to pray!

There are no great volumes of theology you must master before you can pray, no flowery language which you must use, nothing which you must do as a prelude. Prayer is talking with your Heavenly Father, and the conversation should just flow out of your heart.

To learn about prayer as Steinmetz suggested, I would encourage you to get a notebook and divide it into two sections. In the first section, I would make at least four columns: one for the date when you are asking, another for what you are praying about, the third for recording the way God answers your prayer and the fourth for the date of the answer. This, of course, is an encouragement to pray about specific things or situations. Putting the dates down is like driving a stake into the ground so you can measure the distance between the request and the answer.

Now, what about the second section of your notebook? Start reading your New Testament and notice the remarkable promises God has made, promises that tell you that He is a God who hears and answers prayer. When you discover one of these remarkable promises, copy it into your notebook. As you pray, remind God of what He has promised and ask Him to honor His Word.

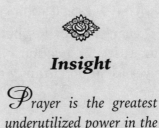

Insight

Prayer is the greatest underutilized power in the world. Find out about it.

God is a gentleman who honors His Word, and though some promises are made specifically to certain individuals or groups, most of the promises regarding answered prayer are simply made to God's children.

An electrical genius believed that prayer offered the greatest promise of reward when it came to scientific research. Would you agree? Or in your personal life is that discovery yet to be made?

Don't wait until disaster or difficulty drives you to your knees in desperation. Learn about prayer by praying. Whether a church, a family or an individual—when someone prays, God's hand reaches out and touches lives. And when He answers, your life will be blessed. It's a truth you can discover for yourself.

Think on This

As you begin working through the selections in this book, don't approach prayer as an "intellectual exercise" but rather as a spiritual journey, getting to know God more intimately, learning for yourself how prayer can— yes, change your life, but more than that—bring you into a deeper relationship with the Father. Look at prayer as an opportunity to learn to say, "Your will be done!"

ＬORD, TEACH US TO PRAY

*"Lord, teach us to pray, as John also taught
his disciples." (Luke 11:1, NKJV)*

Those of you who are familiar with computers know about pull-down menus. When you click on one item, a whole series of possibilities opens up before you. That's the way it is with the fifty-seven Greek words which, translated into English, constitute what we commonly refer to as the Lord's Prayer. Each phrase in this dynamic prayer opens powerful vistas of spiritual insight and potential.

But before we reflect on these words, let's look at the background: One year had passed from the time Jesus was baptized by John in the Jordan River. Luke 11 tells us that in the months the disciples had walked with Jesus they had often heard Him pray, and they were deeply impressed by the fact that His prayers were different from those of the Pharisees. When Jesus prayed, His prayers were warm, intimate and personal, but when the Pharisees prayed, their prayers were cold and impersonal. It was this that prompted the disciples to come to Him with the request, "Lord, teach us to pray. . . ."

Today we need to re-voice the request of the disciples long ago. Prayer for many has become the sending of night letters to God (to use Peter Marshall's expression), or in more contemporary terms, the spiritual e-mailing of our wants and wishes to our Heavenly Father. Prayer is one of the most neglected elements of our relationship with God, without which we remain impoverished and isolated from the warmth of His presence.

When Jesus prayed, His prayers were warm, intimate and personal.

In public, Jesus' prayers were short; in private, quite long. Our prayers tend to be just the opposite—rather lengthy when we wish to impress people but very short or none at all in the privacy of our homes or bedrooms.

In response to the disciples' request, Jesus said,

In this manner, therefore, pray:

Our Father in heaven,
Hallowed be Your name.
Your kingdom come.
Your will be done
On earth as it is in heaven.
Give us this day our daily bread.
And forgive us our debts,

As we forgive our debtors.
And do not lead us into temptation,
But deliver us from the evil one.
For Yours is the kingdom and the power and the glory
       forever. Amen. (Matthew 6:9-13, NKJV)

Now let's begin with that first phrase, "Our Father." First, notice the possessive pronoun *our*. At least seventy-five times Jesus used the term *My*, often saying, *"My* Father." But in praying *"Our* Father," Jesus reminds the disciples that God is the Father of all who have come to peace with His Son through the blood of the cross. When you pray "Our," you step into the fellowship of the disciples who walked with Jesus. You are also in the spiritual company of the Christians in the early Church who met in catacombs. You worship in the same spirit and fellowship of brothers and sisters meeting behind closed doors for fear of the authorities. You are in the invisible company of the redeemed of all ages who have prayed that same prayer.

Insight

The Church of Jesus Christ knows no geographic, racial or temporal boundaries. All who have trusted Jesus Christ as their personal Lord and Savior are brothers and sisters.

Notice too that there is a selflessness in this term *Our*. No *I, Me* or *My* . . . but *Our Father*. Much of our prayer focuses on the fulfillment of our selfish nature instead of searching out the broader path of need for our families, our neighborhoods and our brothers and sisters around the world.

One of the great, undiscovered truths is that the Church of Jesus Christ is a living organism which crosses cultures, oceans, prejudices, languages and barriers. I think it can fairly be said that no nation in the world is devoid of some who name the name of Jesus Christ and pray to the Almighty as sovereign Lord and God. These are your brothers and sisters.

Think on This

1. Does the phrase that Jesus stressed, *"Our* Father," speak to your heart?
2. Have you discovered that, at times, you are closer to a fellow believer whose culture is different from yours than you are, perhaps, to your own siblings?

OUR FATHER

*"This, then, is how you should pray:
'Our Father in heaven. . . . ' "* (Matthew 6:9)

Often we pray words mechanically and perfunctorily and fail to grasp the meaning behind them. How often have you prayed, "Our Father who art in heaven . . . ," without even thinking of what you were saying?

When the disciples came to Jesus and asked, "Lord, teach us to pray," Jesus began by saying, "Our Father." Of all the terms which Jesus could have used—"Almighty God" or "Great Creator" or "Oh Thou, Maker of heaven and earth"—He chose simply to use the word "Father." But what an interesting word, a word that is warm, intimate and personal.

Yet for some that word is troublesome because their earthly fathers have disappointed them. But God is not a man; He is God, and He, unlike some earthly fathers, will never take advantage of you or mistreat you.

In pondering the meaning of that word, notice first that the term *Father* implies a relationship patterned after that which you probably had with your earthly father. Actually all prayer is based on a relationship, the relationship of a son with the Father. In the prologue of the Gospel that bears his name, John wrote, "Yet to all who received him, to those who believed in his name, he gave the right to become children of God" (John 1:12). And to those words add the impact of Paul's words to the Galatians, saying that we are adopted into the family of God. He wrote, "Because you are sons, God sent the Spirit of his Son into our hearts, the Spirit who calls out, '*Abba*, Father' " (Galatians 4:6). As God's children we can call upon our Heavenly Father because we have been adopted into the family of God.

> *He is never so busy running the world that He doesn't hear the most insignificant cry of His children.*

Then notice, secondly, that the term *Father* is a term of reliance. When John F. Kennedy was president of the United States, his son, affectionately called John-John, was very small. Cuba was much in the news, and people were concerned about the missile crisis. The president had called a press conference in the Oval Office of the White House when a side door opened and a little boy wandered into the room. It was the president's son. The press conference stopped as a father put aside the lofty affairs of government because his child needed the attention of his father. That, friend, is a picture of your Heavenly Father's concern for you. He is never so busy running the world that He doesn't hear or have time for the most insignificant cry of His children.

The third thought is that the term *Father* is a term of respect. Periodically I hear God referred to as "The Man Upstairs" or even terms of less dignity. Twice Scripture says that the Lord will not hold him guiltless who takes His name in vain.

Have we lost sight of the awe and even the fear of the Almighty? Has God's name become so common that we no longer care when it is used so profanely? In days of old, the name of God was so holy that ancient scribes would

Insight

Unlike some earthly fathers, your Heavenly Father will never disappoint you or lie to you. He will always be there for you.

not even write that name, but substituted another word lest they be guilty of profaning the holiness of God.

When you pray, remember the warmth which comes through a personal relationship with God as you pray, "Father!"

When John McNeil, the Scottish preacher of another generation, was a lad, he was crossing a mountain pass often frequented by robbers when he heard footsteps behind him. Frightened, McNeil tried to walk faster, but he couldn't elude the person behind him. Finally he heard the voice of his own father saying, "John, it's me—your father." And as you listen carefully you will hear your Father's voice as well.

Think on This

1. In looking back over your relationship with your earthly father, is it hard for you to think of God as "Father"? Why?
2. Ponder the warmth Jesus had for children and realize that He mirrored the same feelings for the children who pressed against His knees as God, our Heavenly Father, has for us.

ᴡHERE IS GOD'S HEAVEN?

*"In my Father's house are many rooms; if it were not
so, I would have told you. I am going there to prepare
a place for you. And if I go and prepare a place for
you, I will come back and take you to be with me that
you also may be where I am." (John 14:2-3)*

"Our Father in heaven . . ." Stop! Just where
is heaven? Literally the words translate
"in the heavens." The space that surrounds planet earth
is really pretty vast, right? Is this what He is talking
about? Yet if you were in China and looked overhead,
you'd be looking the opposite direction of our friends in
Quito, Ecuador. Just where is the dwelling place of the
Father? For a few moments, think with me about how
vast the heavens really are.

In 1977 scientists launched *Voyager II*, a rocket filled
with sophisticated space components, and for twelve
long years it winged its way through space. Then it gradually began to enter the gravitational pull of the planet
Neptune. On the morning of August 25, 1989, cameras
began snapping pictures of Neptune and its moon, Tri-

ton, some 2.79 billion miles in space, showing scenes no mortal had ever viewed before. It took over four hours for pictures to reach us from Neptune, compared with 1.5 seconds for light to reach us from the moon. If, however, you stood on the front porch of Neptune, could you see heaven?

Of one thing we are sure: heaven is a real place, the throne room of the Almighty, and from there God rules in the affairs of men. Jesus told His disciples:

> In my Father's house are many rooms; if it were not so, I would have told you. I am going there to prepare a place for you. And if I go and prepare a place for you, I will come back and take you to be with me that you also may be where I am. (John 14:2-3)

The word Jesus used which we translate "place" is the same word which gives us the English word *topographical*. It was always used of a real place, never a figurative, make-believe place.

Heaven is a real place, the throne room of the Almighty, and from there God rules in the affairs of men.

Some folks have trouble with the question of where heaven is because they're looking in the wrong place. They tend to look for God about like a thief looks for a policeman, and should they actually encounter the physical realm of heaven, they would be greatly upset.

Astronaut Jim Irwin, one of twelve men to actually walk on the moon, said that every individual he talked with who was privileged to go into outer space, including the Russian cosmonauts, was profoundly influenced by what he experienced.

Some of you who read this may be in China, some in India, some in Latin America and some in the former Soviet Union. But no matter where you live, when you go to your local post office, you'll find the flag of your country proudly flying in front, right? The seat of government is in your capital, but wherever you find a post office you find government representation. That's how I think of heaven.

Jesus said, "For where two or three come together in my name, there am I with them" (Matthew 18:20). So where you find a few of God's people, you find that the flag has been planted, and God has brought down a bit of heaven to bless our weary old world.

Think about it when you pray those words, "Our Father in heaven"! And remember, God is unlimited when

Insight

Heaven is God's home, but wherever you find two or three Christians, you find that the Holy Spirit has planted the flag. Jesus is there, bringing heaven to our hearts.

it comes to time and space. Therefore, you can be more certain of heaven than you are of anything on earth.

Think on This

1. It's wonderful when large groups of people pray, but God promised to bless even the prayers of two or three. Does that give you hope?
2. Have you considered forming a small prayer group in your own home or office?

$\mathcal{L}$ET YOUR KINGDOM COME

*"Thy kingdom come. Thy will be done in earth,
as it is in heaven." (Matthew 6:10, KJV)*

$\mathcal{A}$ youth was speaking admiringly of his father when he said, "When Dad's in trouble, he almost always prays." Many of us are like that. As the old aphorism goes, "There are no atheists in foxholes." When you face danger, you are quick to call on the Almighty to get you out of that tough spot! Many of our prayers are filled with personal requests such as, "Lord, give me this and give me that," often asking for financial blessings which we think would solve all our problems.

When the disciples came to Jesus and requested that He teach them how to pray, He mentioned six specific requests. You'll find them all in the prayer we refer to as the Lord's Prayer, recorded in Matthew chapter 6. Of those six petitions or requests, the first three focused on God's rule on earth and had nothing to do with personal needs—Hallowed (or holy) be Thy name, Thy kingdom come and Thy will be done.

The next three requests or petitions were very personal—our daily bread, God's forgiveness for our failures and the request for God's guidance.

In the next two minutes, notice how unselfish were the requests of our Lord. The first thing Jesus asked was for the name of the Father to be holy. Let Your name be holy! A strange request? Possibly, but a necessary one today. We tend to think of a holy man as an odd, out-of-touch individual who drapes a dirty sheet around himself and contemplates religious activities as he lets his beard grow.

Every child of God must make that decision to let God reign supremely in his life and be the rightful King of his heart.

But two concepts are behind the word "holy" that Jesus used: (1) the idea of separation from that which is profane, and (2) purity in a polluted world. Today people know less about the nature and character of God than perhaps any generation, and those same individuals often profane the name of God, almost striving to make it a gutter word, not understanding what they are doing. Jesus says, "Remember, He is a holy God!" which doesn't mean that He is angry or indifferent. His nature and character are without blemish, and He's pure without compromise or corruption.

Then Jesus said we are to pray "Thy kingdom come!" or "Let your kingdom come." What does it mean? First, when you pray "Thy kingdom come!" you are asking God to rule and reign in the affairs of life today. Beyond that you are asking Him to have His way in your own life personally. Jesus told us that "the kingdom of God is within you" (Luke 17:21), which means you must also let the sovereign Lord of the universe reign in your own life personally.

At the present time Elizabeth Regina is queen of Great Britain; but one of these days in all probability Prince Charles will succeed her. He will then become the king. At that time the Archbishop of Canterbury will assemble the royalty and the peers of the kingdom in Great Britain in Westminster Abbey and repeat the words which have been voiced by his predecessors for hundreds of years as he says, "Sires, I present to you your rightful king. Are you ready to pay homage?" Then there will be a thunderous ovation and the Archbishop, as the highest official of the Church of England, will place the crown upon Charles' head. And then he will be the rightful king.

Insight

Jesus Christ is Lord because that is what God has made Him, but allowing Him to ascend the throne of your heart is a decision you make of your own volition.

Every child of God must make that decision to let God reign supremely in his life and be the rightful King of his heart. He never forces His will on you nor overrules your personal will. Yes indeed, "Thy kingdom come. Thy will be done in earth, as it is in heaven" (KJV). So be it.

Think on This

1. If He is to be your Lord, then what does that make you? (A subject of the kingdom? A slave of Jesus Christ [using Paul's term], or someone who wants God's help on his own terms?)
2. Do those who profane God's name in ordinary conversation offend you? Are you ever guilty of the same thing?
3. Does using God's name profanely cheapen His name? Why don't people use the name of Buddha? Or the name of Arnold Schwarzenegger?

ℭHINE IS THE KINGDOM

*"Ask and it will be given to you; seek and
you will find; knock and the door will
be opened to you." (Matthew 7:7)*

When Howard Rutledge was shot down over Vietnam, he prayed for the first time in twenty years. And believe me, it didn't take *another* twenty years for Rutledge to try again. He started praying and praying hard. "When one is dying from starvation," he later wrote of his ordeal, "a bowl of sewer greens is a gift from God. Before every meal during my captivity," he said, "I offered a prayer of thanks."

When Jesus responded to the request of the disciples who had asked that the Lord teach them to pray, one of the things which Jesus said we should pray for is "our daily bread."

Is God really concerned with such mundane things as your daily needs? Nothing is more basic to survival to most of the people of the world than bread or rice. The vast majority of the people in our world are just one meal away from hunger, and that buffer is "our daily bread," or "the bowl of rice" which drives away the gnawing pain of an empty stomach. Our daily bread is a powerful need, and when we pray for our daily bread, God is coming into direct proximity with the fundamental needs of our existence—food, shelter and clothing.

In teaching the disciples to pray this way, Jesus wanted us to understand that the basic necessities of life are not a matter of indifference to our Heavenly Father but a matter of gravest concern. If God is so concerned, why doesn't He just automatically give us everything we need? Good question! Perhaps part of God's reason for prayer is that we can know the answer has come from His hand. Immediately before Jesus gave the disciples this prayer, He said, "Your Father knows what you need before you ask him" (Matthew 6:8), yet Jesus also said, "Ask and you will receive, and your joy will be complete" (John 16:24).

> *Jesus wanted us to understand that the basic necessities of life are not a matter of indifference to our Heavenly Father but a matter of gravest concern.*

Then Jesus taught us that we are to address the issue of seeking and giving forgiveness. "Forgive us our debts," He taught, "as we forgive our debtors." The English Book of Common Prayer uses the word "trespasses," but a comparison with the rendering of the same prayer in Luke makes it clear that we are asking God's personal forgiveness for violating His purpose and will for our lives. This means we are asking forgiveness for sins that we—not others—have committed.

Then we are to pray, "Lead us not into temptation, but deliver us from evil," or put another way, "Lead us not into deep trial, but deliver us from the evil one." Here Jesus is saying we are to pray that we will not be overwhelmed by trials, which would destroy us, but rather that we would be delivered from the evil one.

And finally, we have the words, "For thine is the kingdom and the power and the glory, forever, Amen!" In many Bibles, you will find those words in the margin with a footnote explaining that these words are not found in the best manuscripts.

Insight

When you pray, "Yours is the kingdom," you are bringing your will into harmony with God's purpose and will, individually and corporately. Saying, "Yes, Lord!" always puts you on the winning side.

Well, should we include those beautiful words which seem to spiral upward into the very presence of the throne room of God? Did Jesus say them? Probably not, but did He expect the disciples to pray them? Probably so. And how is that, you may be thinking? The final phrase beginning with the words, "For thine is the kingdom . . ." was the doxology or the ending of all Jewish prayers, and I for one have always felt that Jesus understood that the disciples, as devout sons of Abraham, would add those words.

"Thine is the kingdom . . . thine is the power . . . thine is the glory, forever and ever." What a prayer! Don't wait until you find yourself in great trouble to learn to pray. Begin today with those beautiful words, "Our Father in Heaven," and pour out your heart. That's what prayer is about.

Think on This

1. Have you ever been tempted to think that God is concerned with the "big" things of your life and not the "bread and butter" or "rice and fish" decisions and needs?
2. Do you find your spirits soaring when you pray, "Thine is the kingdom, the power and the glory"? For a moment, think about all three—His kingdom, His power and His glory. Pretty awesome, right?
3. Have you made it a habit to quietly bow your head and thank God for your food, even when you are eating in a public restaurant? Why not start today?

GETTING THINGS DONE THROUGH PRAYER

"Again, I tell you that if two of you on earth agree about anything you ask for, it will be done for you by my Father in heaven." (Matthew 18:19)

General George Patton believed in getting things done. He once told a chaplain, "There are three ways that men get what they want: by planning, by working and by prayer." When rainy, foggy weather stopped the Allied Forces intent on liberating Germany, Patton telephoned the Third Army chaplain and asked, "Do you have a good prayer for weather?"

The chaplain came up with one in a hurry, and Patton had it printed and distributed to the 250,000 men under his command with the order to pray for good weather. "I am a strong believer in prayer," he said.[1] When the weather couldn't be changed by hard work or by planning, Patton resorted to prayer.

Not everyone, however, shares Patton's enthusiasm for getting things done through prayer. A contemporary of the Russian novelist Dostoyevski, whose name was Turgeniev, wrote that "whatever a man prays for he prays for a miracle. Every prayer," he said, "reduces itself to this: 'Great God, grant that twice two not be four.'"

Donald Cole points out that H.L. Mencken used to laugh at prayer. When he signed his letters, "I am praying for you," he considered that to be wildly humorous.[2] I suspect, however, that on his deathbed, Mencken changed his mind.

> *Prayer is conversation.*
> *It has to come out of*
> *your heart, not out of a book.*

As the *Titanic* listed in the icy waters of the cold Atlantic and people began to realize the unsinkable ship was about to go down, the orchestra began playing, "Nearer My God to Thee," and people began praying.

If I had never attempted the broad jump, and I was on a roof with safety a mere six feet away, I can tell you for sure that I would be highly motivated to give the desperate leap my very best try. But if I had trained for the Olympics as a broad jumper, then a six-foot or two-meter leap would be a pretty simple feat. The difference, of course, would be the discipline and training.

That's why one who prays as the ship is going down, or prays at the bedside of a dying loved one, or as a plane tosses in angry clouds is not sure whether his prayer is merely a grasping for a wild hope that God will hear him, or the call of a child who needs his Father's help in the time of danger.

For you who want to discover something of the power of prayer, may I suggest that you start training today. *How?* you may be thinking. Let me put it like this. If I wanted to learn how to acquire a skill, I'd begin by getting some of the best books available and hearing what the experts have to say. If I could get some how-to videos by professionals, I could pick up insights which would help me.

Does that work with prayer? Yes and no. Taking time to study the contents of the prayers which both Jesus Christ and the Apostle Paul prayed gives you a structure, something to use as a guide. There are times

Insight

Prayer is a means of getting things done— God's way.

when I have read some of Paul's prayers—say, those recorded in his letters—and said, "Yes, Lord, that's how I feel. Increase my understanding and give me wisdom. What Paul prayed is what I want and need."

But in the final analysis, you have to learn to pray yourself. Prayer is conversation, remember? It has to come out of your heart, not out of a book. A study of Paul's prayers, however, shows that he prayed about many, many things in all kinds of diverse situations—a practice we need to follow as well. He prayed for others, he prayed for friends, for enemies, for situations, for safety, for deliverance from difficult problems, for physical needs, for deliverance from those who hindered the work. He prayed with other believers in small groups, on his own, in times of worship and praise.

Think on This

1. On a scale of one to ten (with ten being the strongest), how comfortable are you in bringing your needs to God in prayer?
2. After Patton urged the 250,000 men in his command to pray for good weather, the skies cleared and soon their goals were accomplished, thus bringing the fighting to an end. Do you see a cause-and-effect relationship in this? Do you see the same thing between what you pray for and what happens?

1   James H. O'Neill, "True Story of the Patton Prayer," *The Review of the NEWS*, October 6, 1971, pp. 29-31.
2   Donald Cole, "Let Thy Voice Rise," *Moody Radio Program Guide* (Chicago: Moody Bible Institute, Spring 1989).

PRAYER IS A DIALOGUE

*"Again, I tell you that if two of you on earth agree
about anything you ask for, it will be done for you
by my Father in heaven." (Matthew 18:19)*

Conversation is what you make it! It can be as dull as a stockholder's annual report, or it can be as exciting as the news that your husband discovered a lost gold mine!

A lot of our conversation is trivial and rather meaningless. It consists of polite phrases that reek with insincerity, such as, "How are you?" when the person who asked is not any more interested in how you are than in getting a report on the number of Eskimos in the Mongolian desert. Conversation can also be as meaningful and crucial as a midnight phone call to the doctor. It can be necessary and businesslike, or it can lead to a deep relationship, as in friendship or marriage. Of one thing you can be sure: Regardless of the kind of conversation you may have, the fact that there is conversation between two or more persons implies a relationship.

What kind of conversations do you have with God? Perhaps you have not thought about prayer as conversation, but in reality that is what it is. Prayer is simply a conversation between you and God, two persons who have a definite relationship to each other. Perhaps you have only thought of God as an impersonal "it" or a "power." If you've never prayed much, this may explain why. The Bible tells us that God is a Person, not an "it" or a neuter sort-of-reality. It is true that He has a personality different from ours; nevertheless, as a person you can communicate with Him.

> *Prayer is simply a conversation between you and God, two persons who have a definite relationship to each other.*

Can you identify with requests like, "God, I want You to do this and that, and do it real fast because I am in a hurry"? Is that the only conversation you have with God?

How long would you give a marriage when the only thing a husband ever told his wife was, "Get my shirts laundered, have supper ready when I get home and don't be late." Naturally, that marriage would not survive long. Actually, that is not conversation at all. Have you noticed that when conversation ceases, a marriage disintegrates? It is true of your relationship with God as well. When you cease communicating with Him, your relationship begins to disintegrate.

About what should you pray? In one word, the answer is *everything*. It is not my answer; it is the answer Paul gave when he wrote, "in every thing by prayer and supplication with thanksgiving let your requests be made known unto God" (Philippians 4:6, KJV). There is absolutely nothing in life you cannot share with God.

Gordon Cooper, one of the first men in space, tells how he prayed in outer space, thanking God for the glorious privilege that was his and for the greatness of our world. You can do the same on earth.

Ralph Byron, a cancer surgeon, tells how he prays throughout the entire day. He says,

Insight

God's intention is that prayer should be a dialogue—not a monologue.

While I ride to work at the hospital, I breathe a few short prayers: "Lord, help me to do a bang-up job at the hospital. Help me to be a good witness for You." During the day I whisper many short prayers, "Guide me in what I am to say. Watch over me in this operation. Give me wisdom in this problem situation. Thanks for taking care of me."

Prayer is conversation, not just asking, not just demanding something from God. It indicates a relationship!

One last thought: Your relationship to God may be pretty remote. Possibly it may not even exist. But it can. A relationship with God can be established in a moment if you are willing to look up and open your heart to God. Christ came to unite us with a loving Father. Trust Him as a friend and companion, then learn to communicate through prayer.

Think on This

1. British churches often observe a few minutes of silence following a benediction. It's their way of saying, "Hey, take a minute and let God speak to your heart before you go charging out!" Why not learn to do the same thing when you pray? After you have spoken to God, let His Holy Spirit speak to you.
2. Learn to recognize the still voice of God speaking to your heart. That voice will always be consistent with the principles and statements of the Bible. If you have doubt, talk to an older, more mature believer and ask if what you feel God is telling you makes sense to him.

ℭONVERSATIONAL PRAYER

"Again, I tell you that if two of you on earth agree about anything you ask for, it will be done for you by my Father in heaven. For where two or three come together in my name, there am I with them." (Matthew 18:19-20)

*P*rayer, contends Rosalind Rinker, is conversation between you and God. To this woman, whose books on prayer have been translated into many different languages and have passed the million mark in distribution, it's just that simple. As conversation between two individuals who love each other is warm, intimate and very personal, so Ros Rinker believes that conversation with God should be no different.

The fact is, however, that most people haven't the faintest idea how to enter into this kind of a dialogue with God, because the prayers they have heard have been totally different. They have heard individuals—TV evangelists, ministers or priests—pray prayers in a tone of voice and with an intensity that is totally different from normal conversation. They conclude that either

God is deaf or He is so old that He understands Shake-spearean English better than normal, everyday conver-sation.

How did Ros come to grips with this revolutionary idea of praying using short, simple phrases—talking to God as though He were sitting there in the same room? In 1926, at the age of twenty, Rosalind went to China as a missionary secretary. She soon discovered that being a youth as well as a newcomer to a different culture put her at somewhat of a disadvantage with older missionar-ies who were convinced that the way they had always prayed was the right way.

> *When you pray, use short, simple phrases, talking to Jesus as though He were another person in your group.*

One day, Ros was in a prayer group when she heard an older missionary praying about something which Rosa-lind knew had already been taken care of, and so she prayed, "Lord, that prayer has already been answered!" Yes, that frank abruptness disturbed some of the old-timers, but others quickly grasped the importance of complete sincerity in prayer. Out of this developed a concept which has helped millions of people. It is called "conversational prayer."

Here's how it works: two or more people form a prayer group based on the words of Jesus, "Again, I tell you that if two of you on earth agree about anything you ask for, it will be done for you by my Father in heaven. For where two or three come together in my name, there am I with them" (Matthew 18:19-20). Miss Rinker suggests that when you pray, use short, simple phrases, talking to Jesus as though He were another person in your group. She has even suggested that you put an empty chair in your group, talking to Him as though He were actually sitting there.

She suggests that you begin with thanksgiving, focusing on several items for which you are thankful; but unlike formal prayer, the sentences are short. This kind of prayer is a dialogue—not a monologue where someone prays around the world for everything that he can think of. Then, after giving thanks, focus on praying for needs.

Insight

God understands even the thoughts of your heart, so when you pray you don't have to think about how you are going to say something. Just say it.

Does this kind of prayer also work with families and children in particular? Indeed it does. Actually, nothing could be better suited to children than learning to pray conversationally. At your dinner table, everyone enters into conversation, right? You share the experiences of your day with each other and, following dinner, family prayer simply continues the conversation with your

Heavenly Father. Praying this way will change your relationship with God for the better.

Think on This

1. Consider using conversational prayer with your family and encourage your children to use short sentences, praying about only one thing at a time.
2. If you have children, make it a practice that you will never allow the older ones to belittle or make fun of the simplicity of a younger child's prayers.

ℬECAUSE YOU ARE IMPORTANT

"When I consider your heavens, the work of your fingers, the moon and the stars, which you have set in place, what is man that you are mindful of him, the son of man that you care for him?" (Psalm 8:3-4)

hen the astronauts on *Apollo 8* were speeding back to planet earth from their rendezvous with the moon, they reflected on the vastness of what they had seen in outer space by reading the words of the eighth Psalm, where David wrote,

> When I consider your heavens,
> the work of your fingers,
> the moon and the stars,
> which you have set in place,
> what is man that you are mindful of him,
> the son of man that you care for him?
> (Psalm 8:3-4)

You don't have to take a journey into space to be impressed with the vastness of the heavens. But you do have to get away from the lights of the city on a moonless night to look into the vastness of the heavens and marvel at God's handiwork.

It was Israel's shepherd boy-turned-king who wrote the words of Psalm 8. Undoubtedly David spent many a night on the rocky hills of Judea with his father's sheep, pondering the vastness of creation. David probably did not know that the closest star is Alpha Centauri, yet that star is 26 trillion miles away. That's 26 with twenty-one zeros after it, and it takes 4.5 light years (light travels at the speed of 186,000 miles per second) for light to reach us from there. Compare that with light reaching us from the moon in one-and-a-half seconds.

> *God is far more concerned with the inner space of your heart than He is with the outer space of our great universe.*

If you are tempted to feel that you just do not amount to much in the sight of God because of the vastness of the world and the greatness of its population, then try to remember that there is a great deal of difference between space and value. We are overwhelmed by the vastness of creation, yet the vastness of empty space is not as significant as the importance of life.

Think of it in these terms. A very wealthy couple lives in a home filled with valuable paintings and art objects, yet they have no children. One day God blesses their home with a little baby boy—their only child. The nursery is up on the third floor of the great mansion and it is fixed up as nicely as any nursery anywhere. Then one night, the smell of smoke fills the house and the father awakens to realize that his home is on fire.

What is his first concern? The paintings hung on the wall, the lovely works of art or the stocks and bonds hidden in the safe? No, not on your life. He would run for the baby boy in the nursery, because what money can buy is not as important as life—human life. That child is his flesh and blood.

Friend, that is why you were important enough for God to be willing to send His Son to speak to you of a Father's greater love. In Psalm 8, David contrasts man and the Son of Man who came to planet earth. "Son of Man" was a prophetic term which spoke of a coming redeemer who identified with our humanity—His name is

Insight

Never forget that space and value are not the same thing. God values you because you were created by Him and are valuable in His sight.

Jesus Christ. Luke, writing in the New Testament, said, "The Son of man is come to seek and to save that which was lost" (Luke 19:10, KJV).

God is far more concerned with the inner space of your heart than He is with the outer space of our great universe. The created universe—the starry hosts of the heavens—has a message. What God has created speaks of His great power; but the message of the cross speaks far louder, for it speaks of God's willingness to bring us into harmony with His divine will. As David cried, "How excellent is Thy name, O Lord, in all the earth."

Think on This

1. Read about the parables of the Lost Sheep, the Lost Coin and the Lost Son in Luke 15 and notice how valuable the individual is in the eyes of the Shepherd.
2. In reviewing the stories in Luke 15, notice the ratios: a hundred sheep with one lost; ten coins with one lost; two sons and one lost. How does that speak to your heart?

𝒯HE PRIVILEGES OF THE SON

*"Until now you have not asked for anything
in my name. Ask and you will receive,
and your joy will be complete." (John 16:24)*

When the disciples heard Jesus pray, they recognized that His prayers were different from the ones that they had been taught in the synagogue—memorized prayers that they recited over and over. The prayers of Jesus were warm, personal, intimate and couched in simple conversation, and the disciples wanted to learn to pray as He did. "Lord, teach us to pray," they asked, and so Jesus gave to them a model or an example that we have come to identify as the Lord's Prayer.

Jesus taught them to begin their prayer with the simple address of calling God "Our Father. . . ." Unlike some people you hear pray today, Jesus did not bother with the adjectives like "Almighty, immortal, invincible, Thou Great Maker of heaven and earth . . . " and so forth.

God is all of those things and much more, yet Jesus simply used the term *Father*.

When Jesus prayed in the garden and when Paul described the nature of prayer, they both used an Aramaic term for father transliterated as *Abba*. Most modern versions of the Bible do not attempt to give an accurate translation of that word, which was commonly used, but in understanding how it was used we gain some insight into the relationship we can have today with the Father. The Greek word for Father was *pater*, and that is the expression found in the Lord's Prayer. If you introduced your parents to someone, you would show your respect for them by saying, "I would like you to meet my father and mother, Mr. and Mrs. So and So. . . ."

> *It is because of our relationship with the Father that we can come into His presence in prayer.*

But when you go home and close the front door and there is no one there but you and your parents, you might use a different term for your father, calling him "Papa" or "Daddy." It is an expression with warmth and love. That is the equivalent of the Aramaic word which is used in the cry of God's child to His Father.

How about it, friend? Do you have that kind of relationship with God? *Is it possible to have this kind of relationship with God?* you may wonder. *Isn't that being a little too familiar with Him?* No, it is the privilege of a son who is loved by the Father. It is because of our relationship with the Father that we can come into His presence in prayer.

Suppose you went to the palace of a king or a president, and you presented your card and said, "I would like an audience with the king (or with the president)." How far do you think you would get? You might possibly get to the first door or gate, but not much farther. However, the children of the president or the king can come bouncing into their daddy's office because they are related to the chief of state. They need no formal introduction, no appointment. They need observe no protocol. They never worry about saying the correct and proper thing. They simply blurt out what is in their heart. They never bother with "Your Excellency" or "Your Highness!" It is simply "Daddy" or "Father"!

One last thought: your Father knows you far better than you know yourself. He understands the needs of your heart. Matthew records the words of Jesus: "[Y]our Father knows what you need before you ask him" (Matthew 6:8).

Well, if that is true, why bother to pray? If God already knows how I feel and what I need, why bother to tell Him? The Bible also an-

Insight

God's provision for His children brings joy to His heart, just as we are made glad by receiving from the Father's hand.

swers that question. It says, "Until now you have not asked for anything in my name. Ask and you will receive, and your joy will be complete" (John 16:24).

Think on This

1. Look up the context of John 16. Why had the disciples been hesitant to ask for anything? Are we just as hesitant or have we gone overboard in asking for everything we think of?
2. If God does know what we need better than we do, is it not in keeping with the knowledge that He loves us that, on occasion, He says no to what we have asked for?
3. What would happen to our children if we gave them everything they asked for? What would happen to us if God gave us all we asked for?

ƆN THE PRESENCE OF THE FATHER

"This, then, is how you should pray: 'Our Father in heaven, hallowed be your name.' " (Matthew 6:9)

One day a busy father went into his study where he very much wanted to get caught up with some writing deadlines. He had no sooner picked up his pen, hoping to escape interruptions, when his five-year-old son walked in and sat down. Gruffly the father looked up and said, "Well, what do you want, son?"

"Nothing, Daddy," replied the boy. "I just wanted to be where you are."

The boy's father was a famous American evangelist of the past century—Dwight L. Moody, who later told the story to illustrate the fact that prayer brings us into the presence of a loving Father in heaven who is keenly interested in our lives. Later the British expositor G. Campbell Morgan said that it was Moody's story that did more to help him understand the true nature of prayer than anything he had previously encountered.

Said Morgan, "To pray is to be where Jesus is. When we are in His presence, we need nothing more to pray prevailingly." Not bad, is it? In the rush of life today we need to take time to enter quietly into the presence of the Father and to sense that He is right there.

> *Communion with God is the one need of the soul beyond all other needs.*

George MacDonald, the man who greatly influenced C.S. Lewis, sensed something of the strength of being in the presence of the Father when he wrote,

> What if the main object in God's idea of prayer is the supplying of our great, our endless need—the need of Himself? Hunger may drive the runaway child home, and he may or may not be fed at once, but he needs his mother more than his dinner.

Communion with God is the one need of the soul beyond all other needs.

This is one of the truly great yet difficult things to understand about God: that He, in His magnitude, wants to have fellowship with us as His children. To allow us to converse with our Father, we can pray, opening our hearts as we come quietly into His presence.

In many cities of the world the telephone company offers a service which will tell you the time of day. You call a certain number and there is a recorded voice on the other end that says, "At the tone the time will be . . ." However, the voice is cold, impersonal and mechanical. How different from the voice of your father who greets you as you walk into the house at the end of a busy day with tired feet and a weary body. Yet the sound of your father's voice saying, "Hello. How are you?" lifts you above your weariness. That is the privilege that can be yours through prayer.

When Jesus prayed, there was a personal relationship with the Father that His disciples did not have. It was not as though they did not pray, for they did, but their prayers were memorized, mechanical and stale. Contrasting this, Jesus' prayers were warm, intimate conversations with the Father. Listening to the prayers of Jesus, the disciples came to the conclusion that something vital was missing in their prayer life. Quietly they came to Jesus with a request, "Lord, teach us to pray.

Insight

Quiet reflection and meditation make up the kind of prayer that allows the presence of the Father to permeate our souls and to enrich our lives.

. . ." In response to their desire to learn how to pray, Jesus instructed them, saying, "This, then, is how you should pray: 'Our Father in heaven, hallowed be your name'" (Matthew 6:9). He continued giving to them the prayer that Christians have come to know as the

Lord's Prayer. Notice, if you would, those first two words, "Our Father." The first word spans generations and the borders of all nations. It links us in a brotherhood of fellow believers, but the important word is *Father*, for it speaks of a relationship. Prayer is being in the presence of the Father.

Think on This

1. Again, in this selection we have stressed the idea of relationship, which is important in prayer. Does the illustration of the little boy who wanted to be in the presence of his father speak to your heart?
2. Before you pray, take a few moments to just quiet your heart before Him. Then lift your voice in prayer.

℘RAYER IS BASED ON A RELATIONSHIP

"Yet to all who received him, to those who believed in his name, he gave the right to become children of God." (John 1:12)

The adoption of a child is a beautiful expression of love. An adopted child sensed that when he chided his new brothers and sisters, saying, "Mommy and Daddy *chose* me but they didn't have any say about you." When a child is adopted, a parent is willing not only to give love and financial help, but he is willing to give his name to and accept the orphan as his own child. In the first century, there was a Greek expression for adoption called *uiosthesia,* or "the placing of a son."

When a child was adopted in Roman days, he was taken before a judge and three times denied any relationship to his natural father. The third time the judge pronounced him the son of the adopting father. When that happened, he received a new name. If he had committed any felonies or crimes against the state, they were legally wiped out. In a very real sense when a person was adopted, he became a new person with a new identity and with new parents.

That is the very picture that was used by the writers of the New Testament to show what happens when a person receives Christ and becomes an adopted child of God. "But as many as received him," wrote John, "to them gave he power to become the sons of God, even to them that believe on his name" (John 1:12, KJV).

> *As a believer, you can lift your voice in prayer and cry, "Abba, Father." That is the difference between a son and a servant.*

The Apostle Paul discussed adoption in two of his letters, Romans and Galatians. To the Romans Paul said, "For you did not receive a spirit that makes you a slave again to fear, but you received the Spirit of sonship. And by him we cry, '*Abba*, Father' " (Romans 8:15). And to the Galatians Paul wrote, "Because you are sons, God sent the Spirit of his Son into our hearts, the Spirit who calls out, '*Abba*, Father' " (Galatians 4:6).

An exciting picture of adoption and what it means can be found in Lew Wallace's novel *Ben Hur*. In the story, Judah Ben Hur finds himself a slave in a galley ship that is rammed in battle. The next thing he knows he finds himself afloat in the ocean, surrounded with debris from the sinking ship. Ben Hur crawls up on some timber and gasps for breath. Suddenly a body appears in the water. Instinctively, Ben Hur reaches out and drags it to the safety of the flotsam he is on. Ben Hur has saved the Roman tribunal, whose name is Arius.

In time Arius discovers that he has become a hero. Though his ship has been sunk, the fleet that he commanded was victorious, and to show his gratitude, Arius adopts Ben Hur as his own son.

That, friend, is the picture of every man or woman who is adopted into the family of God as the result of what Christ has done. "As many as received Him," writes the Apostle John, "to them He gave the right to become children of God, to those who believe in His name" (John 1:12, NKJV).

Insight

Prayer is not based upon my goodness but upon the fact that I have been adopted into the family of God. Because He is my Father and I am His child, I can pour out my heart with the confidence that He will hear my cry just as an earthly father hears his own child.

A closing thought: When you are adopted into God's family, there are new rights and privileges. Taking advantage of those rights and privileges is not an encroachment on your relationship with the Father; it is simply your inheritance as an heir to the estate. As a believer, you can lift your voice in prayer and cry, *"Abba, Father."* That is the difference between a son and a servant.

Think on This

1. Do you know anyone who is adopted? Is that child loved in as great or greater a measure as natural children?
2. Have you read the book *Ben Hur*? What spiritual truths do you see, based upon the legal application of adoption under Roman law?

ᴛHE PRAYER DIFFERENCE

"You did not choose me, but I chose you and appointed you to go and bear fruit—fruit that will last. Then the Father will give you whatever you ask in my name." (John 15:16)

On the wall of my grandmother's bedroom was a little plaque which bore the message, "Prayer Changes Things!" Dr. Randolph Byrd, a heart specialist in the Coronary Care Unit of the San Francisco General Medical Center, agrees. He's demonstrated that axiom scientifically. Dr. Byrd became curious about the benefit of prayer on patients, so he devised a controlled experiment to see if he could document the effect that prayer had on his patients. Nearly 400 patients agreed to participate in the experiment, whereby the subjects were placed in two control groups without the individual's knowledge of which group he was in. This eliminated the possibility of anyone's saying, "The benefit of prayer is strictly psychological." Dr. Byrd wanted the experiment to deal with physical realities—hard, cold facts.

The medical assessment of the 400 determined that at the beginning of the experiment all of the subjects were pretty much in the same condition physically. Then a group of pray-ers was given only information about the medical problem of individuals in group "A," and were asked to prayerfully intercede for them. They did not know the names of the persons for whom they prayed, nor was there any physical contact between them.

> *God answers prayer because He loves His children and delights in bestowing His gracious favors on them.*

Six months later the results were in. And what happened? Virtually all of those in group "A"—the group prayed for—were physically equal to or in better condition than those in group "B"—the ones not prayed for. But of those not prayed for, twelve required breathing devices or assistance in processing food. Of those in group "A," none required that assistance. Of the group not prayed for, sixteen had required antibiotics to fight infection. Of those in group "A" who were prayed for, three had required the help of antibiotics. Of those not prayed for, eighteen sustained pulmonary edema, but only one-third that number were so afflicted in group "A."

Did prayer make a difference? Those who analyzed the data reported that intercessory prayer "appears to have a beneficial effect" on patients in a Coronary Care Unit. When veteran reporter Charles Osgood reported the finding of Dr. Byrd's experiment, he said, "As we used to say about chicken soup: 'It couldn't hurt.' "[1]

And how do I assess the experiment in intercessory prayer? Interesting, to say the least. I have to note that there is one factor completely missing: What of those in each group who were praying for themselves and what happened as the result of their one-on-one encounter with God?

You see, the Bible says nothing about trying prayer as a "scientific experiment." In fact, theology books are amazingly silent when it comes to a "theology of prayer." Prayer is not something with which you experiment; it's something you do. It isn't like putting a coin in a slot machine when you might hit the jackpot, or buying a few lottery tickets because you might win the lottery.

Insight

Prayer is the most powerful force you can bring to bear upon your family, your neighborhood, your workplace and your world.

Prayer is based upon the relationship of the pray-er with the Father, Almighty God. Galatians 4 and Romans 8 tell us this. God answers prayer not to tip a scientific experiment in favor of the Church, but because He loves His children and delights in bestowing His gracious favors on them. As Jesus put it, "If you, then, though you are evil, know how to give good gifts to your children, how much more will your Father in heaven give good gifts to those who ask him!" (Matthew 7:11).

Learn about the power of prayer. It is still the greatest undiscovered force in the entire world.

Think on This

1. Since the initial study, which I wrote about in this selection, several other scientific studies have documented the effect and power of prayer. But it is the Word of God, not a controlled study, which makes prayer workable. In your own life, ponder the passages of Scripture which you hold on to when you face needs.

2. If you were arrested for being a Christian and held in solitary confinement without a Bible, how many prayer promises would you have stored in your memory? Take the challenge of committing one to memory each week.

---

1   Randolph Byrd, "Positive Therapeutic Effects of Intercessory Prayer in a Coronary Care Unit" [Online]. Available http://www.geocities.com/CapeCanaveral/Lab/6562/SMJ4.html.

$\mathcal{P}$ROGRAMMING

"Then each went to his own home. But Jesus went to the Mount of Olives." (John 7:53-8:1)

ne of the spin-offs of science and technology is the field of programming. As I understand it, in a broad sense the term "programming" applies to putting things together in a logical sequence of events so that each one precedes the other in an orderly progression. And when those events take place in an incorrect sequence, things just don't work. Programming has played an important part in the development of many projects in recent years. Computers have to be programmed. Space programs move in logical sequence. Business plans must be sequential. Programming has almost become a way of life as more and more activities are crowded into a busy schedule.

Many people today have programmed almost every waking minute. They use their appointment books and compress more and more into their waking hours. But eventually programming becomes an enemy and boomerangs on us. Then our strength becomes our weakness. When the traffic light changes and the driver in front doesn't immediately accelerate, we grow short-tempered. We're in a hurry all the time, and the result is that we are programming ourselves to exhaustion. We are tired, frustrated, uptight individuals who are more like animals living in cages than persons who love and feel and respond to others.

Now, before you write off this business of programming, take a hard look at your personal life. How much have you tried to cram into your day? How often do you really get a day off? What advantage is there if you can send faxes and e-mail messages all over the world, see 100-plus channels on television and have options of travel and communication no generation ever had if you have no time for a quiet walk in the woods, no time to smell the flowers or time to romp and play with your children?

The amount of time you take for spiritual enrichment, including time for prayer, gives you an indication of how much value you place on this means of touching God.

Just as you program the activities of a busy life, so must you learn to program time for your spiritual life. For some reason you never *find* that time. You must *take* time to do it. The amount of time you take for spiritual enrichment, including time for prayer, gives you an indication of how much value you place on prayer. It tells you how much or how little you think of this means of touching God.

The problem is not necessarily programming or planning your schedule. It is putting too many activities—and the wrong ones—into our schedules. By His example, Jesus taught us that prayer puts us back in touch with God, with our emotions and with each other. It refreshes the spirit and gives renewed perspective.

Jesus, however, didn't talk about prayer—He prayed! And the contrast between our lifestyles and the example of Jesus is clearly shown in an incident John writes about. Jesus had just spoken to a large crowd of people. "Then," says John, "each went to his own home. But Jesus went to the Mount of Olives" (John 7:53-8:1). Did you notice the contrast? Everyone else went home. Jesus went to a secluded place and

Insight

Ƭhe problem is not planning your time and schedule but not including time for spiritual growth and prayer into your life.

prayed. Often Christ would spend the entire night in prayer, but He never seemed to be weary as the result of losing sleep.

Prayer isn't a concession to your inability to change a situation, but rather the sure knowledge that God is worthy of worship and praise. Prayer keeps you looking up to God, who alone is able to change the status of life. Learn to program time for prayer and you will be a stronger person. John tells us,

> This is the confidence we have in approaching God: that if we ask anything according to his will, he hears us. And if we know that he hears us—whatever we ask—we know that we have what we asked of him. (1 John 5:14-15)

Think on This

1. If this selection has touched on a sensitive place, then revise your schedule. Remember, you are the only one in the world who can do this.
2. Have you ever taken a day—just one day—for a spiritual retreat? Block out a day on your calendar and do it. Take your Bible and spiritual reading materials with you, but most of all, get alone with God and talk with Him.

ℋow Long Should You Pray?

"Be joyful always; pray continually; give thanks in all circumstances, for this is God's will for you in Christ Jesus." (1 Thessalonians 5:16-18)

ℐn my possession is a small, leather-bound book, badly worn and repaired several times over the years. Its printing date is 1848. It belonged to a circuit-riding Methodist minister who happened to be my great-grandfather. Containing many of the thoughts of John Wesley, the little volume was printed primarily to help ministers know how to organize their lives and the churches that they served.

Frankly, it contains a lot of good advice—the kind that would keep a lot of ministers out of trouble if they would only follow it today. The following direction is given to those who preach:

1. Be sure never to disappoint a congregation.
2. Begin at the time appointed.

3. Let your whole deportment be religious, weighty and solemn.
4. Always suit your subject to your audience.
5. Choose the plainest text you can.
6. Take care not to ramble, but keep to your text.
7. Take care of anything awkward or affected, either in your gesture, phrase or pronunciation.
8. Do not usually pray extempore above eight or ten minutes (at most) without intermission.
9. Frequently read and enlarge upon a portion of Scripture.
10. Always avail yourself of the great festivals, by preaching on the occasion.

Not bad advice, even today! That first one—never to disappoint a congregation—means that a minister had better learn to walk on water and leap over tall buildings, because I don't care how talented a man may be, he can't keep them all happy.

Altogether too often, we want to impress people with our piety and drone on and on in a prayer group and pray very little, if at all, in private.

But the one which struck me most forcibly was the instruction not to pray for more than eight to ten minutes in public; that is, leading the congregation in prayer for that period of time. Dwight L. Moody didn't go much for long public prayers. On a certain occasion, a man led in prayer at one of his crusades and prayed on and on. Finally, Moody got up and, somewhat irritated, said, "While our brother finishes his prayer, let's have a song!"

I question whether most pastors today pray even ten minutes a day in private, let alone pray for that length of time in a public service. Should somebody try it today, half the congregation would walk out by the time he finished his prayer.

Studying the prayer life of Jesus reveals something which seems to counter both the advice of the Methodist discipline and what most of us do today. Jesus' prayers were very short in public, very long in private. Altogether too often, we want to impress people with our piety and drone on and on in a prayer group and pray very little, if

Insight

God takes note of our prayers not because of their length, but because of their depth and intensity.

at all, in private. Jesus, however, escaped to the privacy of the Garden of Gethsemane, and there He prayed through the night on several occasions.

He spent the night in prayer before He chose the twelve who were to be discipled. He prayed in the garden prior to the ordeal which led to Calvary. Mark tells us that at the height of His ministry when things were really moving, Jesus withdrew to the desert and there He prayed. Luke says, "Jesus often withdrew to lonely places and prayed" (Luke 5:16).

Have we lost sight of the importance of both public and private prayer today? Has prayer been replaced with program, performance, hype and entertainment? I have a feeling that my great-grandfather, who wore out that little brown leather book, might be pretty uncomfortable with the way we do things today. It's something to think about.

Think on This

1. If you stopped praying altogether, would anything change? What about yourself?
2. Can you not tell a difference in the days when you pray and days when your schedule or whatever keeps you from praying?

WHAT'S ON YOUR PRAYER LIST?

*"You want something but don't get it. You kill
and covet, but you cannot have what you want.
You quarrel and fight. You do not have, because
you do not ask God." (James 4:2)*

For what do you pray? Wealth? Health? Enough
money to meet next month's payments? Or possibly for your daily bread, enough to eat today? Often
our prayers are like grocery orders placed with the Lord.
We tend to do most of God's work for Him ahead of
time and figure out just what we think is the solution to
our needs, then ask Him for whatever we think will
solve the problem. I confess that on occasion the request
for money is attached to my prayers, thinking that with
enough money I can solve most of what I pray about—
without divine intervention.

I have been thinking about the contrast between what
we often pray for and some of the prayers in the New
Testament. One particular prayer is recorded in Paul's

letter to the Colossians. In all probability Paul never got to the city of Colosse, which is located in central Asia Minor about 100 miles to the east of Ephesus. But he did know something about their needs, and he knew an awful lot about prayer and the nature of prayer. After a few words of introduction, Paul told them he thanked God for them every time he thought of them. This is something we do not always do!

> *It is the point of view that makes the difference when you pray.*

Epaphras had come from Colosse to minister to Paul, who happened to be in house arrest at the time in the city of Rome. Here is what he wrote, which, incidentally, is all one sentence in the Greek text.

> For this reason we also, since the day we heard it, do not cease to pray for you, and to ask that you may be filled with the knowledge of His will in all wisdom and spiritual understanding. (Colossians 1:9, NKJV)

He did not pray that they might succeed. He did not pray that they might be blessed with great wealth as a token of their profound spirituality. He did not pray that their kids would fly right. He asked God to give them spiritual wisdom and understanding, and then from this would come a number of things:

1. They would walk in a manner worthy of the Lord and please Him by their lives.
2. They would be strengthened with His might and power so that they might be steadfast, patient and joyful.
3. They might give thanks to the Father who had delivered them from the power or domain of darkness and transferred them to the kingdom of His beloved Son "in whom we have redemption, the forgiveness of sins."

You can see the entire text in Colossians 1:9-14 in your New Testament; and I hope you will take a few minutes to dig it out for yourself.

What strikes me as being so different about Paul's prayer is the fact that he asked that they might fit into God's plan, whereas most of us pray that

Insight

Our Heavenly Father knows best what we need and gives the best to those who leave the choice to Him.

God will fit into *our* plans. There is a big difference. Instead of thinking of God as an office boy who desires this and that for us (while we are still the center of attention, the focal point and recipient of God's help), Paul prays that we might fit into God's plan and purpose and that, knowing Him intimately and personally, we might find His strength and courage to do His will rather than our will.

Have you learned that one of the reasons why our prayers go unanswered is precisely that we attempt to use God rather than ask for wisdom and spiritual understanding? James, the half-brother of Jesus, talks about this in James 4:2, "You want something but don't get it. You kill and covet, but you cannot have what you want. You quarrel and fight. You do not have, because you do not ask God" (NKJV). It is the point of view that makes the difference when you pray. Think about it!

Think on This

1. Seek wisdom that God may guide you in your decisions today.
2. Ask the Lord to teach you how to pray with spiritual understanding.

ᵂHEN YOU PRAY, FORGIVE

"And when you stand praying, if you hold anything against anyone, forgive him, so that your Father in heaven may forgive you your sins." (Mark 11:25)

Of the four Gospels, none is more to the point and straightforward as the account of Jesus' life by Mark. Because of his close relationship with Peter, who himself was a pretty blunt, leave-nothing-unsaid sort of person, many scholars believe that Mark simply reflected Peter's thoughts. With that in mind, may I remind you that some of the most uplifting, positive words of Jesus are also recorded by Mark. For example, Mark tells about the time Jesus was talking with the disciples and said, "Therefore I tell you, whatever you ask for in prayer, believe that you have received it, and it will be yours" (Mark 11:24). Then Jesus said, "And when you stand praying, if you hold anything against anyone, forgive him, so that your Father in heaven may forgive you your sins" (11:25).

Ponder those words, "When you stand praying . . . forgive. . . ." *Just a minute,* you may be thinking. *What does*

God have to do with my relationship with other people? In one word: everything. Prayer reflects a vertical relationship between you and God, but forgiveness is a picture of the horizontal relationship between you and someone else.

Jesus is saying that personal, answered prayer is conditional upon your relationships with others as well as with God. But that's not the way we like it. We prefer to get what we want from God while at the same time snubbing people or holding anger or bitterness against them. But it doesn't work. Immediately after Jesus gave the disciples the prayer we know as the Lord's Prayer, He made this statement: "For if you forgive men when they sin against you, your heavenly Father will also forgive you. But if you do not forgive men their sins, your Father will not forgive your sins" (Matthew 6:14-15).

> *Personal, answered prayer is conditional upon your relationships with others as well as with God.*

Amen!

You can't have it both ways. If you want God's forgiveness, you must learn to forgive others. If you want God to answer your prayers, you have to turn loose your bitterness and let Him deal with some situations.

Why is it so difficult to do this? The answer is that you feel more in control, more in charge when you are filled with anger. But the very opposite is true. We also feel that forgiving someone is a matter of weakness, a giving in to the other, capitulating. But it is none of these. It is turning loose; it is letting go.

The Bible teaches that to forgive someone is to give up your right to hurt that individual who hurt you first. It is also an act of putting the whole situation in God's hands so that He, as the final judge and arbiter of right and wrong, can settle the score for you. It isn't letting the person off the hook, but handing him over to God. And believe me, when you do this, the burden lifts and the anger and hatred in your heart is replaced with God's love.

A rabbi who had lost his family in the Holocaust said that he forgave Hitler for the horrible loss he had sustained—he chose not to bring Hitler to America with him. That's wisdom. In their book *How to Forgive When You Don't Know How,* authors Mary Grunte and

Insight

God finds it impossible to forgive us when we find it impossible to forgive each other.

Jacquie Bishop write, "When you forgive, you reclaim your power to choose. It doesn't matter whether someone deserves forgiveness; *you* deserve to be free."[1]

Should you take time to do a study of how the word *forgive* is used in the Bible, you will discover that in the vast number of occurrences it relates to an individual's response to wrongs that others have done to him, rather than to seeking God's forgiveness for what he has personally done. It includes wrongs done by husbands and wives, by brothers and sisters, by business associates, by neighbors and by friends.

Alexander Pope once wrote, "To err is human, to forgive divine." He was right.

Think on This

1. When someone says, "I'll forgive you this time, but if you ever do it again, we're finished!" has that person really forgiven wrongdoing? Is that forgiveness or probation?

2. Take time to study the context of Mark 11 and underline the words, "When you stand praying, . . . forgive . . ." in your Bible. Is there anyone in your life whom you have not forgiven? What are you waiting for?

---

1 Mary Grunte and Jacquie Bishop, *How to Forgive When You Don't Know How* as quoted by Dianne Hales in "Three Words That Heal," *Reader's Digest*, May 1995, p. 61.

𝒫RAYING WITH THANKSGIVING

*"For everything God created is good,
and nothing is to be rejected if it is received
with thanksgiving, because it is consecrated by
the word of God and prayer." (1 Timothy 4:4-5)*

𝓗ave you ever wondered why some folks bow their heads and pray a prayer of thanksgiving before they partake of a meal and others simply wolf down their food? Where did this practice of praying over a meal come from?

There are two groups who never observe the habit of giving thanks before a meal. Certainly animals never do. They eat whatever is before them, but, of course, animals are animals. The other group is people! People? Yes—but even so, this group is divided into two subgroups: those who refuse to give thanks because they refuse to acknowledge that God has provided for them, and those who refuse to give thanks either out of embarrassment or ignorance.

Where did the habit of bowing your head in a prayer of thanksgiving before you eat a meal come from? It's an old one, going back for centuries. How far, we really don't know. But we do know that Christ and the disciples observed the habit of taking bread, breaking it and giving thanks to God before they ate of it. We also know that this tradition existed in the early Church. Toward the end of his life, Paul instructed Timothy that "everything God created is good, and nothing is to be rejected if it is received with thanksgiving, because it is consecrated by the word of God and prayer" (1 Timothy 4:4-5).

> *Expressing sincere gratitude from a thankful heart is a measure of intelligent worship.*

Bowing your head and rubbing your eyebrows as you mumble, "God is great, God is good, and we thank Him for this food," can be a meaningless routine which is a waste of time and energy. Yet expressing sincere gratitude from a thankful heart is a measure of intelligent worship. It's also the acknowledgment that you are a child of God and recognize Him as the source of all blessings. It is a means of teaching your children something valid and important: Recognizing the blessing and care of God is a mark of spiritual sensitivity and obedience.

"Well, I get embarrassed to pray out loud." Just a minute. Do you get embarrassed to tell the chef in your favorite restaurant, "That was a great meal—one of the best I have ever had"? "That's different!" you say. But is it really?

Prayers of thanksgiving over a meal should be just that. There is a time for real, heart-searching intercession. There is a time to pray for missionaries around the world, for government officials, for your church and for friends and relatives. But this is not the time. Before a meal you say, "Father, thank You for this food. We acknowledge that it comes from You. Please bless it. For this we are grateful. . . ." And that's it.

"OK," you may be saying, "but what about doing this in public?" Every record of Jesus' praying over food was in public—not private. Quietly bowing your head over your food in a

Insight

Every record of Jesus' praying over food was in public—not private.

restaurant makes a statement. So does profanity. So do dirty jokes and suggestive comments. So do bumper stickers.

I have seen people who publicly prayed and prayed, getting louder by the moment. I sat there registering the rise in temperature, feeling embarrassed and out of place—not because I didn't believe in prayer but I felt we were "casting pearls before swine." Yet I think of the

Muslim who spread his prayer rug in the waiting area of a Tokyo airport and prayed. He wasn't embarrassed.

Do you give thanks for your food before a meal? If not, why not? If you are in the group of people who are intimidated by ignorance or embarrassment, it's time to do something about it.

Think on This

Going back to the question which I just asked, have you ever considered the fact that quietly giving thanks for your food—without ostentatious show or creating a disturbance—makes a statement? It says you acknowledge the blessing of God who has provided for you. Can you not do this as an act of gratitude and quiet worship? Begin by doing this with friends.

$\mathcal{A}$NSWERED PRAYER— GOD'S WAY

*"Then they said to the king, 'Daniel, who is one
of the exiles from Judah, pays no attention to you,
O king, or to the decree you put in writing.
He still prays three times a day.' " (Daniel 6:13)*

ishop Winnington-Ingram often told the story of a lad who was hired by a certain farmer to watch some sheep, and when some of his charges strayed, the lad was sent to find them. Being unable to locate the lost sheep and afraid of what would happen because of his failure, the young man decided that he should pray. But he wasn't quite sure how to go about it. That's when a neighbor discovered the lad fervently repeating the alphabet.

"What in the world are you doing?"

"I'm praying," replied the lad.

"No, you are just saying the alphabet."

The lad explained that he didn't really know how to pray, but he thought that if he would only say the letters, God would take them and put them into the right words.

Paul said that God would do just about that. Writing to the Romans, he said that the Spirit helps our weaknesses, for we don't know how to pray as we should, adding that the Spirit Himself makes intercession for us with deep sighs and groaning which cannot find expression in human words.

Praying in the will of God, asking Him for His answer, leaves the door open for God to answer in ways which may surprise you. Our difficulty lies in the fact that we by nature are problem-solvers. We usually wait to pray until we have things figured out. Then we say, "OK, God, here's what I want You to do. Now please do it—fast!"

> *P*raying in the will of God, asking Him for His answer, leaves the door open for God to answer in ways which may surprise you.

God answers prayer four ways. Many answers are *direct*. Frankly, that's the kind I like. Some answers must come right now—tomorrow is too late. In the lion's den Daniel needed an immediate answer as he prayed for God to close the mouths of the lions. Either he had an immediate, direct answer or else he would have been on the menu for breakfast. When you need an answer right now, you can expect God to understand the urgency and respond quickly.

At times, however, answers are *delayed*. Obviously, this is not our first choice. But a delayed answer is not a denied answer. God is simply working out the details, usually in the lives of other people. At times, here at Guidelines, we pray, and seemingly our prayers go unanswered. Then we get down to business and really pray. When the answer comes, coincidence is ruled out. We know without any doubt that God has answered.

But most of the time answers are *disguised* as God responds in a different way, and I look back and say, "God's answer was so much better than mine. This is what I prayed for, and now I can see how much better was His provision." Many of our prayers have money attached to them, and when you pray for valid

Insight

The way God looks at your life is different from the way you look at it. Learn to trust His perspective.

needs, it is never wrong to ask God to meet those needs through His financial provision. Only be sure that you are asking for a need to be met, not simply a want to be satisfied.

Some answers are direct. Some are delayed. Others are disguised. But some are simply *denied*. Is a "No!" answer really an answer? Indeed it is. What a mess our lives would be in if God gave us everything we asked for. Perhaps His answer includes a friend who walks with you through the valley or a period of illness through which you discover His personal presence and power. Perhaps He smiles upon you with a special portion of His grace, which demonstrates how great is His love for you as an individual.

That God hears and answers the prayers of His children is without question, which gives you confidence to trust Him and let Him provide for you in His way.

Think on This

1. Is it possible that what you considered to be indifference was simply God allowing circumstances to come together so that you would know He was the one who made things happen?

2. If you accept the fact that God is sovereign (that nothing happens to His children apart from His will), then you will find it easier to accept the fact that a loving Father, on occasion, loves you too much to answer in the affirmative.

ℰHE FOUR LAWS OF ANSWERED PRAYER

"If you abide in Me, and My words abide in you, you will ask what you desire, and it shall be done for you." (John 15:7, NKJV)

𝒥ust as there are certain physical laws which control the environment surrounding our earth, there are also certain spiritual laws which give definition to prayer. Each one of these laws is a statement or a promise with a condition attached to it, and each one (at least in the original Greek text) contains the word "if," which indicates a condition, something which you must do or meet for God to hear and answer prayer.

Law #1: The law of relationship

In the Upper Room, Jesus taught the disciples, "If you abide in Me, and My words abide in you, you will ask what you desire, and it shall be done for you" (John 15:7, NKJV). There are two parts to this great promise: Abiding in Christ and His Word abiding in you.

It is impossible to abide or to remain in Christ until there is a relationship with God's Son by faith. All prayer is based on this relationship with the Father. The second part is His Word abiding in us, which gives us the direction we need for life.

Law #2: The law of authority

Jesus said, "And whatever you ask in My name, that I will do, that the Father may be glorified in the Son. If you ask anything in My name, I will do it" (John 14:13-14, NKJV). Notice what Jesus didn't say. He didn't say, "If you ask anything in my mother's name, I will do it." Neither did He say, "If you ask anything in the name of the saints, I will do it." He said we are to ask in His name. Praying in the name of Jesus Christ brings His authority to bear on the needs which we have.

Picture a motorcycle policeman who is directing traffic. Along comes a semi-truck, but the policeman blows his whistle. What happens? The truck comes to a rapid halt. Why? Because the little policeman is powerful enough to stop the truck? No! Because of the authority which has been vested in him by the government he represents.

We have not begun to realize what resources are at our disposal by praying in the name of Jesus Christ, exercising the authority which is rightfully ours as His children.

Law #3: The law of divine will

"Now this is the confidence that we have in Him," says First John 5, "that if we ask anything according to

His will, He hears us. And if we know that He hears us, whatever we ask, we know that we have the petitions that we have asked of Him" (5:14-15, NKJV).

Law #4: The law of faith

Jesus taught the disciples,

Assuredly, I say to you, if you have faith and do not doubt, you will not only do what was done to the fig tree, but also if you say to this mountain, "Be removed and be cast into the sea," it will be done. And whatever things you ask in prayer, believing, you will receive. (Matthew 21:21-22, NKJV)

Do you see the condition and the promise, which follows? The condition is asking in faith without doubt. The promise is that God will move mountains, which means doing the impossible.

Martin Luther said that faith is a lively, reckless confidence in God. J. Elton Trueblood

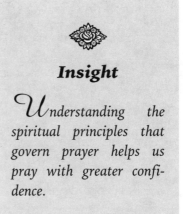

Insight

Understanding the spiritual principles that govern prayer helps us pray with greater confidence.

said, "Faith is not belief without proof, but trust without reservation." To me faith is the assurance that what God has said in His Word is true, and I can act upon it with full confidence that God won't let me down. It's just that simple, but it works. You can make that great discovery for yourself.

Think on This

1. Measure the request that you make against these four conditions, and when they seem to come together with "Yes!" indicators, pray with confidence and expect God to answer.
2. Since God cannot contradict Himself, you can be confident God will keep His promises when you pray them back to Him.

ℱOCUSING ON THE FATHER

*"This is the confidence we have in approaching God:
that if we ask anything according to his will, he
hears us. And if we know that he hears us—
whatever we ask—we know that we have what
we asked of him." (1 John 5:14-15)*

Ignace Paderewski was one of Poland's greatest
pianists. Many great artists have idiosyncrasies,
and Paderewski was no exception. It is said that on the
afternoon before a concert, Paderewski would go to the
building where the concert was to take place. He would
inspect the building, room by room, then return to the
vacant auditorium. There, giving instructions that he
was not to be disturbed, he would sit in silence for several hours. If anyone spoke, he would start the process
all over. In this way the great artist allowed the music to
silently flood his soul. Paderewski knew that he must
have time to concentrate, allowing nothing to distract,
so that the music would eventually fill his heart, and the
overflow would enrapture the audience.

I have wondered just what might be the overflowing of our lives if we could so concentrate and focus on God and let Him work through us. Though you may not have thought much about it, prayer is a means of letting God's presence drown out the dissonant chords of life. It is an opportunity to escape the weary existence of life by coming into the hallowed presence of God. You might say, "Prayer seems strange to me. Imagine talking to Someone you've never met, Someone you don't even know."

> *Prayer is a means of letting God's presence drown out the dissonant chords of life.*

If you have never prayed in your life, there is no need for embarrassment. Every great pray-er had to pray the first time! Some offer their first simple prayers as children at their mothers' knees; another may pray for the first time as emergency medical technicians pull him out of an automobile that has been crumpled like a ball of paper. Some pray their first real prayer in the face of danger, in a foxhole or in a hospital corridor waiting word of the condition of a loved one.

Prayer is never weakness, though it takes the humility of a little child who cries out, "Daddy, please help me." Prayer does not have to be phrased in beautiful words. It should be natural, free, spontaneous. You may talk to God in the same way that you would talk to your closest friend. When you talk to God, do away with the stereo-typed expressions that you may have heard. Be natural, sincere, direct. The prayer that God really hears is the one that comes directly from your heart. If you feel more at ease, pray alone, in a room all by yourself. But remember the important thing is not the words that you say, but is the expression of your innermost heart.

Now, a thought about praying to One whom you have never met personally: Though you have not seen God, proofs of His creative power are all around you. It is possible that you have sensed the touch of God on your life, His protection or His care in ways that are hard to understand. Though we have not seen God the Father, we have seen His Son,

Insight

The dissonant, often troublesome experiences of life are minimized if not eliminated by the warmth of the Father's presence as you wait before Him in si-

Jesus Christ, who came to earth to die for us, God in the flesh. Of Him, John said,

> That which was from the beginning, which we have heard, which we have seen with our eyes, which we have looked at and our hands have touched—this we proclaim concerning the Word of life. (1 John 1:1)

You may not understand it all. It is one of those things you accept by faith just as you do when you pray. And then you find the reality.

Prayer is not a mental exercise to help you empty your mind of troublesome problems. It is conversation with the living God who speaks to our hearts in such a way that the emptiness of our lives disappears.

Think on This

1. Take time to read the short book of Habakkuk in the Old Testament. Notice that after Habakkuk poured out his heart to God asking why, he quietly waited on the Lord, who then spoke to his heart. God will do the same thing for you today.
2. In this modern world, we accept things as realities which we have never seen—such as electricity, the wind, TV signals, etc. Does this make it easier to relate to God?

ℬEYOND "GOD, GIMME THIS . . ."

*"Ask and it will be given to you; seek and you
will find; knock and the door will be opened to you.
For everyone who asks receives; he who seeks finds;
and to him who knocks, the door will be opened."*
(Matthew 7:7-8)

"℧o be a Christian without prayer," said Martin Luther, "is no more possible than to be alive without breathing." Yet the fact is that prayer remains a mystery, an unknown, to many people. Few Christians doubt that, on occasions, people do have prayers answered. Ask people at random if they have either prayed a prayer which was answered or known someone else who had a prayer answered, and the vast majority will answer in the affirmative. Yet many still think of prayer in the same way as they think of putting a coin in a slot machine—doesn't cost much, and you just might hit the jackpot.

I'm thinking of some of the mail which has come to our ministry. One person wrote, "My husband had a friend, a very close friend, who had cancer. I prayed, I fasted, I had my friends pray. . . . Saturday Tom died. What happened?" Another wrote, "I am writing to ask a question. I never get peace of heart. It worries me. Maybe the Lord just doesn't hear me."

A student wrote telling how she prayed before exams and didn't do very well. "My conclusion," she said, "is that probably I lack something in my Christian life."

> *Most of the time we are too proud, too filled with arrogance or doubt, to bend our knees in prayer and say, "God, I need Your help. I want Your will."*

A lot of misunderstanding arises from not knowing the fact that God doesn't answer prayer because we are good—or not-so-good, as the case may be. He answers prayer because of a relationship we have with Him as His children. It's that simple. Paul made that clear when he said, "God sent the Spirit of his Son into our hearts, the Spirit who calls out, '*Abba*, Father' " (Galatians 4:6).

Another misunderstanding is that prayer is just a means of getting things we want—like more money, a better job, a new car, getting people to do what we want, meeting a tall, dark and handsome man or getting someone to like you.

Prayer embraces a relationship whereby you allow God, as your Father, to work His will in your life, trusting Him for what is best; but, yet reminding Him, as He told us to do, of your temporal needs. Jesus said,

> Ask and it will be given to you; seek and you will find; knock and the door will be opened to you. For everyone who asks receives; he who seeks finds; and to him who knocks, the door will be opened. (Matthew 7:7-8)

When Jesus taught the disciples to pray asking for their "daily bread," that specifically means that we can and should pray for our temporal needs, day-by-day.

"Prayer," said George MacDonald, "is not conquering God's reluctance, but taking hold of God's willingness." The problem, most of the time, is that we are too proud, too filled with arrogance or doubt, to bend our knees in prayer and say, "God, I need Your help. I want Your will." That's a humbling experience, but it's what it takes if your prayers are to reach the throne room of the Almighty.

Insight

God is far more willing to work in your life than you are to have Him do so; therefore, prayer is overcoming not His reluctance to do something but our unwillingness to let Him.

One fellow learned that. He was the tail gunner of an aircraft that was drawing heavy fire from the enemy. Radioing for help, he was asked, "What's your position?" He immediately replied, "Kneeling!" He had the right idea.

A final thought comes from the Oxford professor C.S. Lewis. "Prayer," he said, "in the sense of petition, asking for things, is a small part of it; confession and penitence are its threshold, adoration its sanctuary, the presence and vision and enjoyment of God its bread and wine."

Thinking of prayer only in terms of getting things from God means you have not gone beyond the first week in the school of prayer. Keep on praying. There is much, much more to learn about this marvelous relationship, this means of keeping in touch with the Father.

Think on This

1. Why do folks blame God for natural disasters? Have you?
2. For a few moments ask yourself what would happen if God answered all the prayers we pray. Do individuals—say those playing sports—neutralize the prayers of opposing team members? Does God answer the plea, "Help me to win!" as opposed to, "Help me to glorify You and to do my best!"?

$\mathcal{A}$MBROSE WHALEY'S SPIRITUAL SECRET

*"Again, I tell you that if two of you on earth
agree about anything you ask for, it will be done
for you by my Father in heaven." (Matthew 18:19)*

$\mathcal{I}$t happens frequently. The door of my office is closed, and I'm quietly working or engaged in conversation with someone when suddenly the door opens, and a lean, dignified, rather tall American of Norwegian descent—now in his nineties—comes marching in, having done an "end run" around the receptionist and my secretary much as a defensive tackle would in breaking through the line of scrimmage in a football game. In his hand is a magazine article or something encouraging which he thinks will help me. He stays for only a few moments. Then he's gone, often reminding me of Elijah who appeared unannounced in the court of King Ahab.

"Who is that?" people ask.

"That," I explain, "is Armin Gesswein, and he has executive privilege. He's been a dad in the Lord to me for a long time, and he's a very special person." This saint—a real man of God if ever there was one—for more than seventy years has born a name synonymous with prayer, having conducted prayer rallies for Billy Graham's crusades and establishing an organization known as Revival Prayer Fellowship, which brings pastors and Christian leaders together in prayer.

How did Armin learn the importance of prayer?

Armin was a young Lutheran pastor, age twenty-four, striving to plant a church on Long Island, New York, and things were not going terribly well. In his church fellowship was a retired blacksmith, about fifty years his senior. Armin had noticed that when this man prayed, things happened. Armin remembers that "the prayer and the answer were not far apart—in fact, they were moving along together. His 'prayer muscles' were extremely strong because of much exercise." Wanting to learn his spiritual secrets, Armin asked if he might join the old blacksmith in prayer.

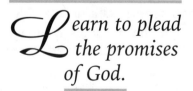

Learn to plead the promises of God.

Going to the blacksmith's home, they crossed the driveway and went to the old barn where they climbed up into the hay loft. Armin prayed. Then Ambrose

Whaley, the old blacksmith, prayed. Finally Armin turned to the old man and said, "You have some kind of a secret in praying. Would you mind sharing it with me?"

"Young man," said the old blacksmith, "learn to plead the promises of God." The old man had knelt between two bales of hay, and on each bale of hay was an open Bible. His two large hands, gnarled and toughened by years of hard labor, were open, covering the pages of each Bible.

Armin learned his lesson well. "I learned more about prayer in that haymow," says Armin, "than in all my years of schooling for the ministry." Now in his tenth decade, Armin Gesswein is still actively speaking, encouraging and exhort-ing. The only heritage which Jesus left the Church, he believes, is a prayer meeting.

Insight

*G*od answers prayer *not because of my goodness or my merit, but because of His promises, which cannot be broken.*

With Armin, prayer is not an appendage tacked on to a planning session or a business meeting. It is the main thing, the frontal assault. He's convinced that one of the reasons both churches and individuals are powerless and overwhelmed with spiritual impotence is that they have not learned the secret of praying: pleading the promises of God.

Understanding the relationship between the promises of God's Word and what we ask our Heavenly Father to do has helped me immensely in my personal life. God honors His Word. Jesus said candidly, "The Scripture cannot be broken" (John 10:35). He also said that the equivalent of crossing a "t" or dotting an "i" would not pass from the law until every bit was fulfilled (see Matthew 5:18).

Learn a lesson from a man who constantly says, "Let's pray!" and he doesn't mean some other time. He means *now!* And then don't just pray, but pray and stand upon the authority of God's Word. Some spiritual secrets are too good to keep to yourself.

Think on This

Have you thought much about the relationship between the promises of God's Word and answered prayer? Begin marking prayer promises in your Bible.

$\mathcal{T}$HE UNDISCOVERED POWER OF PRAYER

"If you believe, you will receive whatever you ask for in prayer." (Matthew 21:22)

$\mathcal{W}$e have a problem and it's got to be solved! So, problem-solvers that we are by nature, we go to work on a solution. Occasionally, all of us feel the need for reinforcement, and that's when we inform God in prayer as to how He should handle the situation. I've discovered through trial and error (and more error than I would like to admit) that quite often my solution is at cross-purposes with God's.

It seems that the early Christians found that a hard lesson to learn as well. Do you recall that crisis in the Church Luke tells us about in the book of Acts, when Herod, the king, killed James the brother of John? Because Herod was scoring political points with the religious establishment, he decided to imprison Peter and eventually execute him as well. The problem was obvious—getting Peter out of prison. In the natural, it was a tough situation. No doubt, they saw four immediate solutions:

1. *They could storm the dungeon.* This would have been glamorous, in spite of being very dangerous, and at the same time, what a publicity coup! How thrilling to show the world that God was with them! "After all," somebody could have said, "the Bible does say, 'If God be for us, who can be against us?' " But that idea wasn't practical. Sixteen soldiers guarded Peter. Two were chained to each wrist. Too difficult!

2. *They could have circulated a petition.* Not a bad idea. After all, don't Christians have rights too? No doubt the petition could have been done quite effectively, since there were thousands of Christians at that time, and some pretty popular people had identified with the cause. But the Holy Spirit didn't impress this on their minds.

3. *They could collect money and bribe Herod.* Human nature doesn't change much from generation to generation. For centuries, men have opened doors by greasing the palm with gold instead of putting oil on the hinge. Politicians were corrupt then too. But God never leads His children to violate what He has written in His Word, so rule that out.

4. *They could hold a public demonstration.* Why not picket the prison and talk about justice? Peter had done no wrong, and the government did ensure certain rights, but public demonstration wasn't the answer.

How did the early Church attack this problem? If they thought of the solutions which I just advanced, we have no record of it. Luke tells us they called a prayer meeting. How illogical!

Or was it? Luke says, "But the church was earnestly praying to God for him" (Acts 12:5). How the enemies of the cross must have laughed. "We've got their number one man in the slammer," they jeered, "and what do they do but pray!" They soon realized, though, how effective prayer can be. Contrary to all reason and human logic, God heard that prayer and unlocked prison doors to release Peter—even to the surprise of those who prayed.

Perhaps you are facing a difficult situation right now. In the natural you are trying to figure out how to solve it. God's way may be totally different from yours. Why not let Him solve it as only He can? Prayer is not doing "nothing at all," as some think of it; it is submitting your problem to the will of your Heavenly Father, who is limited by nothing. It is the most powerful, positive course of action available to men and women today.

Insight

Prayer still unlocks closed doors and frees the captive.

Long ago, Lord Alfred Tennyson wrote, "More things are wrought by prayer than this world dreams of." It is true today, friend. And it's still the greatest undiscovered power in our world.

Think on This

1. Was there ever a situation more hopeless than that which confronted Peter? Think of the security of sixteen soldiers guarding him. Now ponder your own need. Is it greater than that which confronted Peter?

2. How do you account for the servant girl's apparent surprise when she opened the door and saw Peter? Isn't that what they were all praying for? Honestly, are you sometimes surprised when God does answer your prayers? Why?

$\mathcal{M}$Y HOUSE WILL BE CALLED A HOUSE OF PRAYER

"My house will be called a house of prayer, but you are making it a 'den of robbers.' " (Matthew 21:13)

"$\mathcal{E}$xcuse me, pastor, could I ask when your people come together for prayer in your church?" As a visiting speaker, I used to ask that question from time to time. No longer! I kept getting answers like, "Oh, our men meet for a prayer breakfast on the sixth Saturday of each month!" or "We have a ladies' prayer group that meets in the basement every Thursday morning." I began to sense that I had asked an embarrassing question akin to "How much are the gold fillings in your teeth really worth?"

It isn't that I totally fault the pastors. Many of them believe in prayer, and I'm sure they pray personally. But a lot of them get the feeling that prayer meetings and funerals have two things in common: Few people attend and everybody is glad when they are over.

When Jesus went one-on-one with the men who had turned the temple into a local merchandise mart, he defiantly cried, "My house will be called a house of prayer" (Matthew 21:13).

Was Jesus making a statement which in reality should be a standard by which we evaluate the spiritual life of the Church today? Should churches be houses of prayer? Should prayer be the identifying mark of a group of believers?

What's happened that prayer has become part of the professional rhetoric of the individuals who stand in the pulpit and lead in worship, but so divorced from the ordinary life of the Church?

Wherever you find spiritual awakenings today, you will find people who pray.

Is there a relationship between the lack of corporate prayer in churches today and the spiritual impotence which is so prevalent? The story is told that Thomas Aquinas once was shown through the Vatican treasury. The pope said, "Well, Thomas, no longer can we say, 'Silver and gold have we none.' "

"Yes," replied Thomas, "and no more can we say, 'In the name of Jesus, rise up and walk.' "

Not all churches, however, have missed the connection between prayer and power. Wherever you find spiritual awakenings today, you will find people who pray.

Dr. Billy Kim is pastor of the large Central Baptist Church in Suwon, South Korea. My friendship with Billy goes back to college days when we used to barnstorm together in Youth For Christ rallies. When Billy met me at the door of their new church to show me the new facility, he said, "Follow me," and started up several flights of stairs. I thought it strange that he first didn't take me into the large sanctuary which is filled several times each Sunday morning. Instead, he showed me some twenty small rooms just large enough for a person to kneel and pray in.

"This," said Billy, "is the secret of our church." He explained that these were prayer closets where people pray twenty-four hours a day, seven days a week.

Insight

God always honors the prayers of His people, but prayers unprayed are prayers unanswered.

Is there a relationship between the growth of the Korean church and prayer? It is no coincidence that almost every Korean church, regardless of its denomination, has an early morning prayer meeting every day of the year where people begin the day by praying, often kneeling on concrete floors.

But that wouldn't work here! you might be thinking. Oh, yeah? Don't believe that voice for a moment. There's a new breath blowing today—the breath of God's Spirit calling men and women to prayer. A prayer movement is touching the lives of churches and study groups, revitalizing them, giving them spiritual vigor and power.

If Jesus really meant that His house should be a house of prayer, and our churches are known for anything but prayer, we've fallen short of what He expects. Think about it.

Think on This

If you have no regular prayer meeting in your church, first pray about the situation, then approach your pastor and ask if he would consider starting one with your help.

Prayer—both spontaneous, individual prayer and group—prompts and brings the moving of God's Spirit. Make sure the meeting is for prayer, not a time to castigate your church for being insensitive and callous to the need for prayer.

ᗯHY NOT?

*"Husbands, in the same way be considerate as you
live with your wives, and treat them with respect
as the weaker partner and as heirs with you of the
gracious gift of life, so that nothing will hinder
your prayers." (1 Peter 3:7)*

ᕼave you ever wondered why at times your
prayers go unanswered when you have prayed
specifically for something? A man asked me that question
a few days ago. His brow was knit with worry. He was a
top-notch insurance salesman with an infectious smile,
but like a big-league batter in a slump, he just could not
seem to break out of the doldrums. He prayed and worked
hard, but the hard work and prayer just did not produce.

Like a doctor who begins to poke and prod a patient, I
began to ask some probing questions. "Is there anything
that you know of which has short-circuited your relationship with God? Is there any bitterness between you
and anyone else? You know," I continued, "the Bible
says if we regard iniquity in our hearts the Lord will not
hear us" (see Psalm 66:18).

He thought for a minute and then said, "No. None of these are problems that I can think of."

Then I asked, "How are things in your marriage?"

He paused for a moment and asked, "What does my marriage have to do with answered prayer?"

"Oh," I said, "First Peter 3:7 says that one of the reasons our prayers go unanswered is because of unresolved conflicts between a husband and a wife."

"Really!" he responded. "I don't think I ever saw that."

Noticing his look of surprise, I turned to First Peter 3:7 and shared the exact words where Peter wrote, "Husbands, in the same way be considerate as you live with your wives, and treat them with respect as the weaker partner and as heirs with you of the gracious gift of life, so that nothing will hinder your prayers."

> *Very often God answers prayer just a bit differently than we think He should.*

As I shared those words I could see light had dawned. My friend was excited. "I didn't know that trouble at home could keep your prayers from being answered." Then he looked puzzled as he said, "Well, that's not it. We have a good marriage. Everything's OK there."

I thought I had found the answer, but I hadn't. So I asked, "Are you asking God for your needs or your wants? James 4:3 tells us that at times our prayers go unanswered because we ask selfishly."

"Man," he said, "I have not had a sale for almost two months! I'm hurting!"

How could I explain a situation like that? I said, "There are times when we just do not have the answers. All I can tell you is that there are times when we have to keep on praying and trusting Him. Suppose the two of us join in prayer and ask God to let you sense His presence and, during this period of trial, help you to trust Him even more." I prayed not

Insight

Learning to trust God regardless of circumstances is the greater lesson of prayer: the one Jesus taught us in Gethsemane by praying three times, "Not my will but thine be done."

only that he would break out of his selling slump, but also that God would teach him a greater lesson—the lesson of trusting Him regardless of the circumstances. I have discovered that very often God answers prayer just a bit differently than we think He should.

An unknown author wrote,

> I asked God for strength that I might do great things;
> I was made weak that I might learn humbly to obey.
> I asked for health that I might do greater things;
> I was given infirmity that I might do better things.
> I asked for riches that I might be happy;
> I was given poverty that I might be wise.
> I asked for power that I might have the praise of men;

I was given weakness that I might feel the need of God.
I asked for all things that I might enjoy all things;
I got nothing that I asked for, but everything I had hoped
    for.
Almost in spite of myself, my unspoken prayers were
    answered.
I am among all men most richly blessed.

A few days later I saw the businessman who had come to me. "How's it going?" I asked.

"Better than ever," he replied, "but what I really learned through all that was to trust Him regardless of business."

What better lesson is there to learn?

Think on This

1. A friend who is a new Christian seems to experience immediate and definite answers to prayers. You are an older, more mature believer and seemingly you don't experience the same, immediate answers—at least, all of the time. How do you explain this? Is it a phenomenon which often happens?

2. Is God answering prayers only when "business is good" and things are going well? Have we confused prayer with simply "getting things from God" instead of worshiping Him and bringing our wills into conformity with His?

𝒫RAYING IN THE WILL OF GOD

*"The LORD is good, a refuge in times of trouble.
He cares for those who trust in him." (Nahum 1:7)*

𝒫 rayer is not demanding things from God, nor is it manipulating God to do what you want. It is more than simply asking and receiving, though in prayer we do ask and receive. Prayer is more than an SOS when you are in difficulty. It is communion, conversation between you and your Heavenly Father; but unlike so many of our conversations with people which are superficial and trite, prayer with our Heavenly Father should be intensely personal, deep and meaningful.

I've come to the conclusion that prayer doesn't change God's will nearly as much as it changes mine, bringing my stubborn will into conformity with the will of the Father. And when I want what God wants, things happen which otherwise would not. John, who walked with Jesus as one of the twelve, wrote, "Now this is the confidence that we have in Him, that if we ask anything according to His will, He hears us" (1 John 5:14, NKJV).

Now, most of the time you know what to pray about. Jesus taught the disciples to pray, "Give us today our daily bread," which tells you to pray about the daily needs of your family and personal life. When a member of your family is not a believer, you can pray in the will of God for his conversion, because Scripture says God is not willing that any should perish but that all should come to repentance (see 2 Peter 3:9).

When I want what God wants, things happen which otherwise would not.

But what about the times when you just don't know what God's will is? How do you pray then? Good news, friend. It's found in Romans 8:26, where Paul addressed this very issue. He wrote, in essence, "We do not know what is right to pray for, but the Spirit Himself intercedes for us with groanings too deep for words," or, translated differently: "The Spirit Himself intercedes for God's own people in God's own way."

Beautiful! Paul's words became especially meaningful to me when my mother, then in her eighties, was diagnosed with cancer. I asked myself, *Should I pray for her recovery? Should I pray for a quick homegoing? Should I simply pray for God's grace?* No, I earnestly asked God for His will with the comfort that He already knew, and the

Spirit Himself would intercede according to the will of the Father!

Not sure how to pray? Pray for the will of God, which is to pray in the deepest level of faith. You can trust God to provide and answer in His way, which is far better than just trying to figure it out yourself and then inform God of your solution.

Paul says the Holy Spirit helps our weakness or infirmity. The word "weakness" was used three ways in Scripture:

Insight

The Holy Spirit makes intercession for God's children according to the will of the Father, which means you don't have to figure out just what God needs to do.

1. It was used to describe physical illness or sickness. Paul used the word when he instructed Timothy to take some wine for his stomach's sake and frequent illnesses.

2. It was also used to contrast strength. A ball team riddled with injuries plays from a position of weakness, not strength.

3. It indicated a moral flaw or tendency to yield to what we know is wrong. Paul says when we are like that, God's Spirit, who has come to indwell our lives, intercedes with the Father on our behalf.

OK, you don't fully understand it. Neither do I, but it isn't necessary for you and me to fully understand it, provided we can trust it. It is far better to have weak faith in a strong plank than strong faith in a weak plank; and I suspect your experience this far has indicated that God will honor the promises of His Word so we can rest in the confidence that God knows what is best and will meet us as we trust Him. A final thought: Prayer is not overcoming God's reluctance to help; it is overcoming our stubborn refusal to let Him work His will in our lives as His children. Think about it.

Think on This

Do the words of Paul bring comfort to your heart as they have mine? Were you ever in a situation that had you completely at a loss as to how to pray?

$\mathcal{I}$F GOD DOESN'T ANSWER PRAYER

"Ask and it will be given to you; seek and you will find; knock and the door will be opened to you." (Matthew 7:7)

$\mathcal{H}$ow do you answer those who say that prayer seems to work for some but not for others? Take, for example, the story told by Kathryn Porter in her book, *Ship of Fools*. The boat is about to sink and the people gather on deck to pray; nonetheless, the ship eventually flounders and goes down. That question of why prayer works for some and not for others was on the heart of a listener who wrote the following:

I am inclined to write to you because I feel I have lost my faith. To make it short, let me say I've been praying constantly over the past year for a financial blessing. How can I believe in God and Christ when nothing happens to me and my prayer? Maybe I'm doing something wrong. I'm about to give up on the whole situation.

For the next three minutes, let's assume that God does not answer prayer. What would be the implications? First, what would we do with the many passages which tell us that God hears and answers prayer? Like what? Like Matthew 7:7, where Jesus said, "Ask and it will be given to you; seek and you will find; knock and the door will be opened to you."

One of my favorite passages is Mark 11:24, where Jesus said, "Therefore I tell you, whatever you ask for in prayer, believe that you have received it, and it will be yours." Obviously, Jesus would be asking us to do something which is an exercise in futility if God doesn't hear and answer prayer.

> *He wants us to ask so that we may know the answer has come from His hand.*

Then what of His own example? Jesus spent long hours in prayer in the Garden of Gethsemane. It was a vineyard, not a place of relaxation or even a place of beauty, but a place of solitude where He could escape the press of the crowd and the weariness of a busy life. He also told us that we "ought always to pray, and not to faint" (Luke 18:1, KJV).

Then what of the examples of believers down through the ages? Study the biographies of men and women who have made their mark for God, and you will find normal human beings who have learned the lesson of prayer and have prayed much. Prayer and power go hand in hand.

In Seoul, Korea today, you will find the largest Presbyterian church in the world, the largest Methodist church in the world, the largest Assembly of God church in the world and several other churches numbered among the largest churches in the world. You will also find men and women who are convinced that prayer works to the point of rising at 4 to 5 a.m. and meeting together for prayer.

The implications of saying prayer does not work are far greater than explaining why God, at times, chooses not to answer prayer. In the book of James, the writer addresses this very issue and gives us some powerful insights as to why some prayers are unanswered. He says, "When you ask, you do not receive, because you ask with wrong motives, that you may spend what you get on your pleasures" (James 4:3).

Insight

Explaining why God does not answer all prayers the way we would like is not nearly as difficult as explaining why He should answer anyone's prayer at all.

The purpose of my writing this book is to give you insights as to how prayer works, so that you may pray and know that your prayers are heard. God is far more interested in answering your prayer than even you are in asking Him for something. He said, "Ask and you will receive, and your joy will be complete" (John 16:24); and even though He knows what we need before we ask, He wants us to ask so that we may know the answer has come from His hand. It's just that simple.

Think on This

1. How prevalent is the popular theology which seems to picture God as a "sugar daddy" or the Great Santa Claus of the sky who gives anything we ask for? What would you say to someone who believed this theology?

2. On occasion, God does answer the plea of a desperate person; however, the relationship of a son—as opposed to that of a stranger—makes all the difference. If you are uncertain that you are a son of God, then take time right now to invite Jesus Christ into your life and claim Him as your Lord.

   Read Revelation 3:20 and personalize it, recognizing that He will come into your life and forgive your sins. Then do the same thing with John 3:16. After you have done this, tell someone. That's like drawing a line in the sand and stepping across it, never to return to your former status or lifestyle.

PRAYER IN CHURCHES

*"Again, I tell you that if two of you on earth
agree about anything you ask for, it will be done
for you by my Father in heaven." (Matthew 18:19)*

An axiom in mathematics is that if your premise is incorrect, your conclusion is bound to be wrong as well. Use the wrong formula and the answer is certain to be incorrect. That logic applies to a host of things, including the operation of a local church. Having equated activity with spirituality, the average church today has a calendar filled with a multitude of activities, most of which are well and good, but which leave little room for the disciplines that produce spiritual change in the lives of those who attend.

Take, for example, the place of prayer in a local congregation. Of course, churches believe in prayer, yet the prayer meeting in many groups has been replaced by activities that range from craft classes to organized sports.

I am thinking of the time I ministered in churches in Korea—dynamic churches where people meet for prayer early in the morning, seven days a week. One Sunday as I was about to speak in a worship service in an American church, the pastor reminded me, "Be sure to stop by 10:15 a.m. so our people can have their coffee on the patio. You know our coffee time is important."

> *The tragedy is not that we do not believe in prayer; rather, it is that we do not pray.*

Somewhat annoyed, I replied, "Yes," adding, "and that is the big difference between Korean churches and churches here. They seem to be powered by prayer, while we are fueled with coffee." No, there's nothing wrong with a cup of coffee and fellowship, but what is often wrong is our priorities.

Even a casual reading of the New Testament, especially the book of Acts, illustrates the direct relationship between the power of God and the practice of corporate prayer in the Church. The infant Church was born in a prayer meeting. When challenged by authorities, the disciples immediately regrouped and prayed. When Peter was imprisoned, it was prayer that opened the door. When it came time for Paul and Barnabas to take the first missionary journey, it was with prayer and fasting that they were sent forth. Writing to a young man who was a pastor to Gentiles, Paul said, "I urge, then, first of all, that requests, prayers, intercession and thanksgiving be made for everyone" (1 Timothy 2:1).

Our failure to make prayer a priority in the church body results in our spiritual impotence. The average church bulletin looks more like a medical report on the aged and infirm than the charter of men and women who believe God hears and answers prayer. But the average church today is so far beneath the norm which God intends that to rise to the spiritual level of the early Church makes it appear abnormal.

If the Christian life is spiritual warfare, which the Bible constantly stresses, and if we are to survive individually and collectively as a body, we must rediscover the power of corporate prayer. We must avail ourselves of the weapons of our warfare which Paul discussed when he wrote to the Corinthians. We must

Insight

Talking about prayer and praying are two different things. What we do affirms what we really believe.

use the weapons of our warfare to pull down the strongholds of the wicked one. *The tragedy is not that we do not believe in prayer; rather, it is that we do not pray.*

When the pastor reacted somewhat negatively to my comment about churches being fueled with coffee, he was quickly silenced and changed the subject when I asked, "By the way, when do you pray as a church body here?" If you are a pastor, rethink your priorities from God's standpoint. If you are a lay person, take inventory of your personal life.

Remember, like those who met in the home of John Mark, you can start a prayer group in your home. "Where two or three are gathered together in My name," Jesus told the disciples, "I am there in the midst of them" (Matthew 18:20, NKJV). And if He is at your prayer meeting, what more do you need?

Think on This

1. In the previous selection, I urged you to get involved in some kind of a prayer group. If distance makes this impossible, what about a prayer chain by telephone or by e-mail?
2. Check with your pastor about specific needs he would like you to pray with him about.

PRAYING FOR YOUR PASTOR

*"Pray also for me, that whenever I open my mouth,
words may be given me so that I will fearlessly make
known the mystery of the gospel. . . . Pray that I may
declare it fearlessly, as I should." (Ephesians 6:19-20)*

Visualize an old man as he slowly makes his
way to the top of a hill overlooking a valley
where two armies are about to go into battle. Then as
the conflict begins, the bearded old patriarch raises a rod
toward his army. As long as he extends that rod like a
magic scepter toward his army, they win. But his arms
eventually tire and the rod sags toward the ground. Immediately the tide of battle turns, and the enemy begins
to push back his army. But then two of the old man's as-
sistants come alongside him and hold up his hands.
Again the old man's army starts winning.

Strange, is it not? But it actually happened. You can
read about it in the Old Testament book of Exodus,
chapter 17.

Moses, the leader of God's children, was the patriarch, and Aaron and Hur, two of the priests, came alongside him and supported his hands in victory. Here's the biblical account:

> So Joshua fought the Amalekites as Moses had ordered, and Moses, Aaron and Hur went to the top of the hill. As long as Moses held up his hands, the Israelites were winning, but whenever he lowered his hands, the Amalekites were winning. When Moses' hands grew tired, they took a stone and put it under him and he sat on it. Aaron and Hur held his hands up—one on one side, one on the other—so that his hands remained steady till sunset. So Joshua overcame the Amalekite army with the sword. (Exodus 17:10-13)

Truth is always stranger than fiction.

When you pray for your pastor, God touches his heart and life, and his message then touches the hearts of people.

In their book *Power House*, authors Glen Martin and Dian Ginter suggest that the incident of Exodus 17 provides a model for praying for Christian leaders today. Why not pray for your pastor instead of just getting rid of him? First, note that the best of men are but men at their best. Moses got tired; so does your pastor. Moses didn't walk on water. Neither does your pastor. Then notice that Moses couldn't do it all by himself. Neither can your pastor—no matter how motivated he is, no matter how hard he works. Two men had to come alongside Moses and hold up his hands. These two men, Aaron and Hur, men whose names are not as important as Moses', were the key to victory.

Please also observe that Moses didn't go into a prayer closet. He went up on the top of a hill where everybody could observe him. A Christian leader is like a man in a fish bowl. He has no secrets, and what he does—either good or bad—influences all kinds of people. "Moses climbed to the top of the hill for two reasons—insight and inspiration," say Glen Martin and Dian Ginter.

Insight

Prayer strengthens those destined for failure or misfortune and allows them to succeed in an otherwise hopeless situation.

When you pray for your pastor, God touches his heart and life, and his message then touches the hearts of people.

When J. Wilbur Chapman was a young pastor, several people came to him and said, "Mr. Chapman, we have had other pastors in this church who were better preachers than you are, and in time they failed. We think you will probably fail too. However, we are going to pray for you." And pray they did—earnestly, fervently—that God would bless the life and ministry of this young man.

And what happened to Chapman? He became a powerful evangelist through whom thousands of people came to a saving knowledge of Jesus Christ.

Wherever you find men and women who accomplish anything for God, whether it is a lonely patriarch with his arms outstretched toward the army of Israel, or a country preacher or missionary laboring in a forgotten place, you will find people who pray.

Think on This

Behind every successful pastor is someone who prays. Would you consider being a prayer supporter for your pastor? For a missionary supported by your church? For your son or daughter's teacher at school? If you answer yes, then take the second step and let that person know that you will stand behind him in prayer.

ASK CHRIS MILBRATH IF PRAYER MAKES A DIFFERENCE

"Is any one of you sick? He should call the elders of the church to pray over him and anoint him with oil in the name of the Lord. And the prayer offered in faith will make the sick person well; the Lord will raise him up." (James 5:14-15)

When Chris Milbrath was working with Co-Mission in the Ukraine, the last thing that he ever thought would happen to him was a trip to the hospital for surgery. At the time, Chris was twenty-five years of age—a handsome, healthy, strong specimen of young manhood. He's six feet, five inches tall with a shock of blond hair and is endowed with the kind of good looks that turns the heads of young women.

But then, unexpectedly, a stomachache didn't go away. It had to be more than indigestion. Eventually a doctor told him, "You've got a ruptured appendix, and unless you have surgery immediately, you're going to die." A second opinion would have been comforting, but the hospital where Chris was hadn't paid their phone bill, and the phone had been shut off. Calling for another appointment was not an option.

Surgery took place the next day. It didn't go well. Infection threatened his life. A roommate who understood a little English said that he prayed and praised the Lord in his delirious stupor.

Then, halfway around the world, an older woman, a friend and supporter, suddenly woke in the middle of the night. She felt an irresistible burden to get out of bed and pray for her young friend. She didn't know why. She just knew that she should pray. Later as they compared notes and made adjustments for the difference in time zones, Chris and the friend were amazed that this strange prayer burden came at the very time his life was hanging by a thread.

> *The Bible makes it very clear that there is a link between prayer and the recovery of sick people.*

What happened? Within twenty-four hours, word got through to a medical missions group in Moscow that things hadn't gone well and that the hospital didn't have the resources or equipment to save his life. A small jet just happened to be available and was sent to airlift Chris to Geneva where one of the best surgeons in Swit-

zerland was available for additional surgery which undoubtedly saved the life of this young man.

As Chris shared his experience with me, he was preparing to going back again to serve in the same city
where he went through this trauma. I couldn't help
wondering what might have happened if that woman
had turned over and said, "I'll pray for Chris tomorrow."

"Well," you say, "God could have awakened someone else." Of course, and God isn't restricted in His pur-
poses by people who don't answer a wake-up call in the middle of the night. What He wants done, He's going to do.

But when something like this happens, sev-
eral powerful things come together. First, there is no questioning the fact that there is a link between prayer

Insight

*God can do what He wants done apart from in-
tercession; nonetheless, God often prompts us to pray so that we may know the correlation between His work and our prayers.*

and the circumstances which led to Chris' recovery. The
Bible makes it very clear that there is a link between
prayer and the recovery of sick people (see Mark 16:18
and James 5:14). Then there is joy on both ends, knowing that someone played a part in the redemptive work
which God wanted accomplished. Do you remember

how Jesus said, "Ask and you will receive, and your joy will be complete" (John 16:24)?

There are those occasions when God does prompt someone to pray specifically for a person in time of need, but don't wait until you are jolted from a deep sleep with an urgency to pray before you intercede for those who are serving the Lord.

God's work, as well as His workers, are energized by prayer. The measure of our accomplishment is really the reflection of the prayer base supporting those of us who are involved in His work. Make prayer for others a vital part of your support. Your prayers make a difference. Chris Milbrath knows for sure.

Think on This

1. It doesn't take vast numbers of people praying to move the hand that moves the world. Better than waiting for God to prompt you to pray, single out one or two individuals you know and pray regularly for those people—whether they be friends, acquaintances or missionaries.

2. Have you ever had a specific prayer burden for someone? Have you ever shared that burden with the one for whom you prayed?

*T*HE POWER OF
THE BENDED KNEE

*"This is the confidence we have in approaching God:
that if we ask anything according to his will,
he hears us." (1 John 5:14)*

*G*eorge Mueller was educated in the universities of Germany during the period of time when rationalism was the dominant philosophy. Rationalism is a humanistic philosophy that leaves God pretty much out of life, and Mueller certainly did that very thing for the first twenty years of his life. As a young man, Mueller's life consisted of wine, women and song. He ended up in jail, to the disgrace of his father and family, who wanted their son to become a clergyman. Mueller wanted anything but that!

At the age of twenty, while studying at the university, he was invited to the home of a friend who was a Christian. That evening Mueller was intrigued to see his friend kneel and pray—an act Mueller had never seen before. At his home following the meal, the host read a chapter from the Bible—the same one that one of Mueller's professors had earlier ridiculed—and the reading of Scripture was followed by a hymn. Mueller felt so awkward that he apologized for even being there, but that night changed his life. Mueller was shortly thereafter converted to Jesus Christ. After his conversion, he quickly learned the secret of prayer.

> *We need to rediscover the power of the bended knee—the power of prayer.*

In the university, Mueller had excelled as a scholar. With the same fervent dedication, he now turned to the Scriptures and began to apply them to his life. Rejecting a rationalistic approach to life, Mueller believed that faith is believing the promises of God and then standing on them completely. At the same time, Mueller began to be concerned for the orphans who wandered the streets of Bristol, England, where he was pastor. This was the beginning of the orphanages Mueller established, which were operated on the principle of faith in God.

During his lifetime, George Mueller never asked for money for his work, yet in response to his faith, God sent in the equivalent of well more than $1 million. There were times when there was no food, yet Mueller would not allow his staff to send out an SOS for money—unlike some organizations today. Instead, he would go into his room and bend his knees in prayer.

Often, he would instruct, "Set the table for dinner," although there was nothing to cook, and then he would go to prayer . . . and God provided.

The power of the bended knee—in a world of missiles and bombs measured in megatons, a world where so much that happens (even in the Christian realm) is a result of good promotions and clever psychology. We need to rediscover the power of the bended knee—the power of prayer.

When Mueller was in his eighties, he was asked to speak to a group of seminary students. One of them raised his hand as the old man finished his address. He said, "Mr. Mueller, there is a question some of us would like to ask."

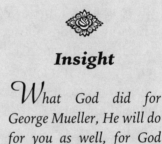

Insight

What God did for George Mueller, He will do for you as well, for God has no respect of persons.

"Yes," answered Mueller as he strained to hear.

"What is your secret?" the youth queried.

The eighty-year-old man pushed his chair back and began to bend his old limbs to the floor as he knelt in prayer. *"This is the secret,"* replied Mueller.

One of his biographers wrote that when Mueller died, it was discovered that there were two grooves worn into the wooden floor by his bed. Mueller had literally worn two depressions into the wooden floor with his knees as he knelt beside his bed in prayer.

The God of George Mueller is yet alive and well today, and He still answers prayer. May God help us to discover the power of the bended knee.

Think on This

1. Do you think that the manner in which God answered prayer—without vocal financial appeals and four-color promotional pieces—was something special for just Mueller? Do you think that God will meet those involved in His Word the same way today?

2. Hudson Taylor, a friend of Mueller, used to say, "God's work done God's way will never lack God's supply." Do you agree?

3. How many ministries do you know which make no financial appeals?

𝒫RAYING AS A COUPLE

*"Finally, all of you, live in harmony with one another;
be sympathetic, love as brothers, be compassionate and
humble. Do not repay evil with evil or insult with insult, but with blessing, because to this you were called
so that you may inherit a blessing." (1 Peter 3:8-9)*

𝒥f you have never prayed with your husband or
wife, I must ask, "Why not?" More than a few
times I have asked couples that question, and I get a
wide variety of answers. I often get the feeling that people feel awkward or clumsy praying together. In some
cases they think that prayer is a private matter or that it
belongs in church, or they feel embarrassed to pray together. But once a couple learns what prayer can do for a
relationship, they change and change quickly.

Don't forget that God already knows everything about
you, everything that takes place between you and your
mate—and between you and everybody else, for that
matter. There are no surprises with Him. You've also
got to remember that, when you are His child, God loves
you far more than you can imagine.

If you've never prayed together as a couple, I have a suggestion. Sit at a table with an empty chair and think of prayer as a simple conversation between you and Jesus Christ. Talk to Him as though He were actually sitting there. By the way, hold hands when you pray. There's something about touching each other as you touch God that makes for powerful chemistry.

You can pray together at any time, but unless you pray together at some particular time of the day, you'll probably not make prayer a habit.

> *When a couple will agree to pray together—no matter what has happened, from infidelity to poor communication—they are moving toward a solution.*

For many years my wife and I have made our time of prayer the first thing in the morning. I'll often stagger downstairs and make a pot of coffee, and by then Darlene manages to join me. We will often drink coffee together and pray, one voicing thoughts in simple phrases, then the other.

What can prayer do for a couple? Plenty! It can open the door for effective communication, help you to address issues that could tear you apart, help you find God's power in your personal lives in ways that you would never discover otherwise, give you wisdom in knowing how to parent, how to cope with the problems of work and how to stay on top of circumstances.

Recently I was talking with a couple who have all but given up on their marriage. Four children, ages six to fourteen, are involved. The father doesn't want a broken home. Neither do the children, but unless God does something, their marriage is history. "How long has it been since the two of you have prayed together?" I asked.

They looked at each other, and the husband said, "I don't know." Thinking for a moment, the wife replied, "It's been at least four years."

For most of those years, the couple had been in counseling. A lot of hours and more than a little money had gone into saving that marriage, but not once in the past four years had they joined hands and said, "God, You know what is happening to our lives, and we

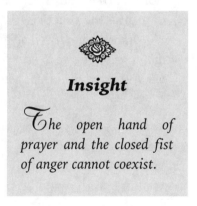

Insight

The open hand of prayer and the closed fist of anger cannot coexist.

don't like it. We need Your help. Help each of us to be the person You want us to be, and forgive us of sins and failures."

When a couple will agree to pray together—no matter what has happened, from infidelity to poor communication—they are moving toward a solution. But in closing I must warn you of something. There is danger involved in prayer. It can upset your agenda, but it can bring healing and hope for a better marriage. The danger is well worth facing.

Think on This

1. If you are single, are you comfortable praying in the presence of others? What does your response tell you about yourself? about others?
2. If you have never prayed together as a couple, suggest to your mate that you take thirty days and make this a trial period. If, at the end of that period, you both do not feel that your lives have been enriched, then discontinue the practice.

   Author's note: If you do give up on prayer, feeling that it didn't help, I'd like to hear from you. You would be the first one I've ever heard from who could honestly say that.

CRAYER THERAPY AND MARRIAGE

*"Our help is in the name of the LORD,
the Maker of heaven and earth." (Psalm 124:8)*

Does prayer make a difference in a marriage? Sociologists believe it does. Surveys of married couples done in conjunction with the Gallup Poll and the National Opinion Research Center confirmed that when people pray together, they have a far greater chance of dealing with problems that cause the marriages of others to crash and burn. Prayer doesn't eliminate all the problems, but it does give individuals a means of coping with them.

The surveys reveal that seventy-five percent of couples who pray together say their marriage is "very happy" compared to fifty-seven percent of those who never pray. Inversely, fifty-eight percent of those "who are not very religious," have serious marital problems, compared with forty-five percent of those who describe themselves as religious. It also appears that prayer—

rather than the frequency of sex in marriage—is the most accurate predictor of marital happiness. This news, of course, will cause hundreds of unhappy couples to start praying together every day, right? Probably not, though I wish that were true.

Why don't we pray? Pride, stubbornness, possibly ignorance. There is, however, a powerful therapy to prayer when a couple will come together once every day, clasp hands and pray using simple, everyday language and terms, talking to God as though He were the third party of a conversation, possibly even visualizing His presence by putting an empty chair in the room.

What does prayer do for a couple and what are the benefits of prayer therapy?

Benefit #1: Prayer reduces us to the same level

The issue of power—who is in charge—is one of the most frequent causes of marital battles. But when you pray, you are on equal footing. It's somewhat humiliating, as well, because prayer forces us to recognize that God is sovereign and we are human. As David cried out, "As a father has compassion on his children, so the LORD has compassion on those who fear him; . . . he remembers that we are dust" (Psalm 103:13-14).

Benefit #2: Prayer brings an arbitrator, a referee, to the table

Prayer lowers the emotional temperature. Arguments are gradually diffused as you say, "Lord, we look at this issue differently, but we want Your will. What do You want us to do?" Having prayed together, couples talk—which brings us to the next benefit.

Benefit #3: Prayer is the key to communication

You can pray standing up, sitting down, lying down or on your face before God. But when you pray with your mate, I suggest you join hands in an expression of oneness. It's hard to be angry when you vent your emotions openly and honestly before God. Prayer drains the bitterness from your heart, which then enables you to communicate, to talk about what really concerns you.

Insight

Prayer—sincere, earnest prayer—is a powerful force in turning around a troubled marriage.

Benefit #4: Prayer therapy changes your heart and mellows your spirit

The benefit here is not saying words without meaning, but meaning what you say—which then gradually helps you to change your life.

Benefit #5: Prayer results in intimacy and sexual fulfillment

It's a fact according to valid research: The greater a couple's religious commitment, the more satisfying is their sexual relationship.

Over the years I have challenged thousands of couples to put the entire issue to a thirty-day test. Agree together that for just thirty days you will take a few minutes every day and pray together. I am convinced that if you take the thirty-day test, you'll never stop.

Think on This

1. If you are married, ask your husband or wife to read this segment, then bring up the subject of taking the thirty-day challenge.
2. In your prayers, talk to God as if He were physically present, with full understanding that He knows exactly what has been going on in your life.

$\mathcal{P}$RAY AND GROW RICH

"This is the confidence we have in approaching God:
that if we ask anything according to his will,
he hears us." (1 John 5:14)

$\mathcal{H}$ow to Pray and Grow Rich! There was the title in bold print, advertising something that compelled you to read the fine print in the ad. The pitch began, *"This offer may be the most important event of your entire lifetime!"* Now that sounded exciting. I read on: "In this book you will discover how to pray and grow rich, and I promise you immediate results," says Dr. Joseph Murphy. The table of contents read: "Your Right to Be Rich. The Three Steps to Riches. How to Pray and Grow Rich. Where to Discover a Gold Mine. The Multi-million-dollar Formula."

It is not that I am an unbelieving sort of skeptic. But with the price of the book what it was, I began wondering, *Who really grows rich—the person who reads the book or the author!?*

I know quite a few people who seem to do a lot of praying. Some specialize in prayer, but for some reason I am left with the impression that they are not exactly rich. When I am with them, I suspect that they have never heard about Mr. Murphy's book.

I know another fellow who should have had the book. His name was Peter. He was a fisherman. Luke, in Acts 3, tells us he was on his way to the temple to pray when a lame beggar stopped him. Peter had to tell him, "Silver and gold have I none" (3:6, KJV). But I like what Peter did tell him, which indicates something of the real—not the prostituted—nature of prayer. Peter said, ". . . but what I have I give you. In the name of Jesus Christ of Nazareth, walk" (3:6). And Dr. Luke tells us that the lame man did just that.

*P*rayer speaks of a relationship with God, made possible by what Christ did.

In the years that I have spent studying for Master's and Doctorate degrees in Bible, I cannot remember a single reference from Scripture that says anything about "praying and growing rich." I do remember that Christ once commented on the effectiveness of poverty programs. Candidly He said, "The poor you will always have with you" (Matthew 26:11). Jesus said a great deal, though, about prayer and its effectiveness.

There is a school of thought today which suggests that prayer is kind of an inside pull with God, a string-pulling, a kind of technique that gets you whatever you desire. Such a concept wholly misinterprets the nature of prayer and what the Bible says about prayer. Prayer is not just a plea of "gimme's—gimme this and that"—any more than your relationship with your earthly father is constantly, "Gimme some money, Dad."

Prayer is communication with God. The disciples came to Christ, and He sat them down beside blue Galilee and taught them. He said, "After this manner therefore pray ye." He began saying, "Our Father which art in heaven, Hallowed be thy name" (Matthew 6:9, KJV).

Insight

Prayer produces spiritual riches which take us far beyond the material.

Prayer speaks of a relationship with God, made possible by what Christ did. Of Himself, Christ said, "I am the way and the truth and the life. No one comes to the Father except through me" (John 14:6). Again Christ said that our requests should be directed to God in His name. He said, "You may ask me for anything in my name, and I will do it" (14:14). Paul said that our requests should be made to God with thanksgiving (Philippians 4:6). That is not a bad idea!

For what are you thankful? The next time you feel led to ask God to make you rich, I suggest that you sit down first and count your blessings. Begin to thank God for what He has already done. Thank Him for the prayers that have already been answered, and I think you will begin to realize you are already rich. You will realize the riches that really count are not those that are kept in a bank vault. They are the riches of health and happiness, children, character and influence. Well, didn't Jesus say "a man's life consisteth not in the abundance of the things which he possesseth" (Luke 12:15, KJV)?

Think on This

1. When we were living in the Philippines, my daughter once asked, "Daddy, how come when we are here we are so rich and when we go home we are so poor?" Take time to count your riches, not your wealth. Make a list of the five most important blessings you can count.

2. Can you relate to the man who said, "So what if they fire me! I still have my wife and children, my integrity and a place to sleep. All they can do is take my paycheck and I'll trust God for our needs"? What enables someone to be so confident? Could it be they know that God really is in control?

$\mathscr{H}$AVING CONFIDENCE WITH GOD

*"And this is the confidence that we have in him, that,
if we ask any thing according to his will, he heareth us:
And if we know that he hear us, whatsoever we ask,
we know that we have the petitions that we desired
of him." (1 John 5:14-15, KJV)*

"Whenever a Chinese tries to tell a Westerner about Chinese temples and worship, he soon finds himself saying that it is all very confusing," says Joyce Savidge in her book about the temples of Hong Kong. More than 600 Chinese temples are found in Hong Kong. Half of them are Buddhist and about an additional one-third are Taoist, the rest a mixture of both. "Many worshipers," says the author, "look on both religions as though they are one and the same. They are unable to say whether this belief is Buddhist or that statue is Taoist. And they are just as uncertain about their own position, often settling for Buddhism because it is best known. Others cannot put a name to their religion at all. They say that they just worship their ancestors and the gods."

Within the temple is a beaker-like container known as the *chim* containing either 64 or 100 thin slivers of bamboo, identical in length, about the dimensions of a chopstick; however, there is one difference: each one is numbered at the top. When a person needs guidance, he will go to the temple and while kneeling before the vessel will shake it until one drops to the ground. A priest then reads the number and interprets the message—for a small fee, of course. Take your pick: numbers one to a hundred. But many of the Chinese of Hong Kong do not put much faith in the "numbers game."

What oxygen is to the lungs and food is to the body, prayer is to the soul of man.

Their real god, they say, is the god of wealth, and they have a panoply of deities connected with money: one dealing with salaries; another with gambling, of course, to make you lucky; another who copes with debts, etc. In reality the god they acknowledge is not a real person but a mystical influence connected with their ancestors. What a contrast to the clear assertion of the Christian that God hears and answers prayer!

San Hey Seng, the Cambodian who has translated some of our Guidelines programming into his language, was born the son of a silversmith who made idols for the

Buddhist temples of Cambodia. At the age of twelve, young Lem Cheong, as he is known to his friends, went to his uncle, who had been a Buddhist priest for many years, and asked, "Uncle, have you ever prayed to Buddha and Buddha answered your prayers?" Somewhat taken aback by the brashness of the youth, the uncle nevertheless admitted that he could not remember any definite answer to prayer which he directly attributed to Buddha.

Later the young man put the same question to a Christian and Missionary Alliance missionary: "Can you ever remember praying to God and He answered your prayer?" Quickly the missionary responded by recounting several answered prayers. So impressed was young Lem Cheong that he became a Christian

Insight

Just as there are physical laws that control our universe, so are there spiritual laws which control our relationship with God and how He responds to our prayers.

that very day. Over the years Lem Cheong has never considered prayer to be a "numbers game," as those do who take their pick and try to spiritualize some meaning. Prayer to him is vital, personal communication between God's child and his Heavenly Father.

How is prayer with you? Is it a "numbers game"—taking your pick and hoping for a positive response? Is it like putting a coin in a one-armed bandit? Or is it conversation between you and God? What oxygen is to the lungs and food is to the body, prayer is to the soul of man. It is vital to the growth and spiritual prosperity of a Christian.

"And this is the confidence that we have in him," wrote the Apostle John, "that, if we ask any thing according to his will, he heareth us: And if we know that he hear us, whatsoever we ask, we know that we have the petitions that we desired of him" (1 John 5:14-15, KJV). This is the positive assurance of God's Word.

Think on This

1. Would you serve a "deity" who never answers prayer? So many people do. Why?
2. Romans 10:17 tells us that faith comes through hearing or understanding the Word of God; therefore, the more you know of the Word, the greater will be your faith. Begin a list of prayer promises which you create as you read Scripture. Add whatever insights you have as you master these.

ᘐRAYER FOR A MISSIONARY IN TROUBLE

"Are not all angels ministering spirits sent to serve those who will inherit salvation?" (Hebrews 1:14)

he bulletin of the World Center for Missions relates the following story. A medical doctor serving in a small field hospital in Africa had to go to a nearby city twice a month for medical supplies, including drugs for the patients. While he was there, he would withdraw money to pay the staff and provide for living expenses. The distance was too far to cover in one day, so each time he made the journey he would stop overnight.

On one trip, he encountered two men who were fighting; and one of them had been injured rather badly. Seeing that the one was quite badly hurt, he treated his injury, completed his business and then returned home.

In his own words,

Two weeks later I repeated my journey. Upon arriving in the city, I was approached by the young man I had treated two weeks earlier. He told me that he had known that I carried money and medicines. He said, "Some friends and I followed you, . . . knowing that you would camp overnight. We were waiting just outside your campsite for you to go to sleep. We planned to kill you and take your money and drugs. But just as we were about to move into your campsite, we saw that you were surrounded by twenty-six armed guards."

At that the doctor laughed, assuring the young men that he was entirely alone. But they were positive. There were five of them, and they all counted twenty-six. Realizing that they were hopelessly outnumbered, they were fearful and fled.

Don't wait to make prayer for missionaries and Christian leaders a priority on your time, but include your pastor and others you support in prayer each day.

When the missionary doctor returned to his home church, he related the incident during a service, and as he told the story, a man jumped to his feet and interrupted. "Sir, can you tell me the exact day that this incident happened?" This caught the doctor by surprise, and he had to stop and think, but he was able to remember the exact date.

Then the man who interrupted him told his story. He said that there is a time differential of about twelve hours between his home and the medical clinic in Africa. On that very morning as he was putting his golf clubs in the car to go play golf, he felt a prompting to pray for this very man. He felt it so strongly that instead of going to the golf course, he went to the church and got on the phone. He called as many men as he could, and they came that Saturday morning and prayed for the medical doctor in Africa.

He finished his story and said, "Would all of those men who met with me on that day please stand up?" They stood. And when they counted them, the number was exactly twenty-six!

Does the Holy Spirit, on occasion, prompt us to pray for one another,

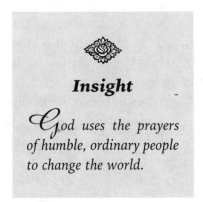

Insight

God uses the prayers of humble, ordinary people to change the world.

especially in times of great need? Of that there is no question. But I do know one thing for certain: When you have your golf clubs in hand, ready to head for the first tee, there has to be a very certain voice to cause you to cancel those plans and head for the church to pray! Don't wait until then to make prayer for missionaries and Christian leaders a priority on your time, but include your pastor and others whom you support in prayer each day.

Does it make a difference when people are upheld in prayer? Having experienced that myself, I can tell you that there is a tremendous difference. Things come together. God honors His word and you connect with the needs of people. Prayer is not an exercise in wishful thinking. It is conversation with our Heavenly Father, and in praying for each other, we become part of the harvest, part of the solution. It is our privilege and responsibility.

Think on This

1. Take a concordance of the Bible and do a study of angels and in particular those angelic beings whom God sends to protect His own.
2. Angels are popular today. We have TV shows and dozens of books reminding us of the existence of supernatural beings. Do you think these detract from biblical truth or add to it?
3. Have you ever been in a situation in which you suspect an angel was involved?

A SPONTANEOUS EXPLOSION OF PRAYER

"Then they returned to Jerusalem from the hill called the Mount of Olives, a Sabbath day's walk from the city. When they arrived, they went upstairs to the room where they were staying." (Acts 1:12-13)

*A*lmost 250 years ago, Jonathan Edwards wrote a book about the great spiritual awakening which was shaking the world of his day. In his book this godly man made a fascinating prediction. He predicted that the prayer movement would accelerate in subsequent generations climaxing around the year 2000 A.D.

Why, in the year 1748, theologian and preacher Jonathan Edwards chose the year 2000 is uncertain at this point. But of one thing we are sure: Today there is a global prayer movement which is touching the lives of Christians all over the world.

David Bryant, founder of Concerts of Prayer International, writes,

The last 10 years have seen significant developments in the international prayer movement. We have seen an increase in prayer mobilizers bent on drawing the church together within their cities. We have seen the emergence of community-wide pastors' revival gatherings. We have seen new prayer thrusts in denominations and Christian organizations. The prayer movement is finding new expressions.

Bryant is not alone in recognizing that what is taking place is a global phenomenon. Church historian and statistician David Barrett, an Episcopalian, says that approximately 170 million Christians are committed to praying every day for revival and world evangelization. He believes that some 20 million people feel a definite calling to make prayer their priority ministry.

The universal, spontaneous quickening of our hearts with the Almighty is one of the most promising signs we have seen on the horizon in our generation.

For something to be a real movement of God, there has to be an element of spontaneity which goes beyond individuals trying to organize people and get them to do something. Has that been true of what is happening today? Absolutely! The prayer movement today is touching schools, churches, groups of pastors gathering together, office personnel, factory workers, friends who meet together, prayer circles, churches who adopt other churches half a world away and what have you. People are agreeing to pray by phone; by day and by night; march for prayer (praying for cities as they go); pray in churches, businesses, coffeehouses, at work and wherever they can meet. Says Bryant, "All this activity suggests that we are in the vortex of what may be the most significant prayer movement in the history of the church."

I personally believe that the universal, spontaneous quickening of our hearts with the Almighty is one of the most promising signs we have seen on the horizon in our generation. "Whenever God is ready to do something new with His people," wrote historian J. Edwin Orr, "He always sets them to praying." Dr. Orr, whose specialty was the study of religious awakenings in history, knew that prayer always preceded a movement of God's Holy Spirit, revitalizing the body of Christ.

Insight

History tells us that individuals who dedicated their lives to prayer made a difference in the impact of a revival or spiritual awakening.

What will prayer do? Prayer will energize your own spiritual life and put you in touch with the power of God. Prayer is conversation between you and the Father, and you cannot pray without sensing His response in your life. Then prayer will energize your church.

Prayer will revitalize your marriage as well. It is virtually impossible for a marriage to fail when two people pray sincerely and earnestly for the will of God in their lives.

When it comes to people who believe in prayer, there are but two kinds: those who believe in prayer but do not pray, and those who believe in prayer and pray. These are the ones who are changing our world.

Think on This

1. Have you been guilty of minimizing the impact of your prayers, thinking that you are just one person and not a very important one?
2. The 10-40 window is a designation for large groups of people who are yet unevangelized. Find out who some of those people are and begin to include one or two groups in your daily prayers.

ℛEES HOWELLS

*"Then Jesus went with his disciples to a place called
Gethsemane, and he said to them, 'Sit here while
I go over there and pray.' " (Matthew 26:36)*

ees Howells was born on October 10, 1879,
the sixth of eleven children born to a couple
in a little mining village in South Wales. You've never
heard of Rees Howells, right? I'm not surprised.
Howells will never be remembered as a world leader, a
politician, a scientist or a great educator, though he was
one. He was a missionary, the founder of a Bible school
in South Wales, and a participant in the revival which
shook the little country of Wales.

But most of all, Howells carved his niche in the church
of his day as a great man of prayer, an intercessor who
prevailed with God on behalf of others. Howells believed what Paul wrote, that "the weapons of our warfare are not carnal, but mighty through God to the
pulling down of strong holds" (2 Corinthians 10:4,
KJV).

Howells was not the kind of person who went to a prayer meeting and then dozed off, calling that prayer. No, he spent many long hours and days in prayer, often praying day after day for the same need. Then, having finally heard from God, with the exactness of an Old Testament prophet, Howells would rise from his knees and announce that God had heard him and that what he had been praying for would happen. Time and time again, the circumstances would bear him out. The events would unfold exactly as he stated.

> *In his lifetime, Howells trusted God for literally millions of dollars for ministry. His simple faith was based upon the promises of Scripture.*

As a young man, Howells became dissatisfied with the lot of the men who worked the mines in southwest Wales and decided that he could emigrate to the U.S. and become rich. He came to the States and began to make money but still was not satisfied. Though he attended church, he was not a believer. Through the persuasion and encouragement of a friend he was converted and returned to his native Wales where he began to work in the mines.

For the next few years, God began dealing with him in a very direct manner. The desire for money had to go, along with the desire for leadership and prominence.

Gradually, God began to show him that He would be his sufficiency. Repeatedly, Howells gave away his savings, asking God to meet his needs—which began a pattern of living by faith.

Though he knew and was influenced by George Mueller, whose ministry was that of intercession for orphan children, Howells never attempted to duplicate anyone else's ministry. He felt that God called him to intercede in prayer, and that giving his life in intercessory prayer was the reason for which God had laid His strong hand on him and had called him to serve Him.

In his lifetime, Howells trusted God for literally millions of dollars for ministry. He never presumed upon the Lord. His simple faith was based upon the promises of Scrip-

Insight

The example of Rees Howells demonstrates that God can use anyone who will trust Him and take the promises of His Word personally.

ture. "The promises of God," he said, "are equal to current coin." He didn't believe in going into debt with the anticipation that God would bail him out. Instead, he earnestly prayed, quoting Scripture to God, reminding Him of His promises. When God had supplied three-fourths of the funds for a project, he began building or moving ahead, trusting God for the balance, which always came together.

Though I don't necessarily believe that the lives of people such as Rees Howells or George Mueller should be an example for everyone to follow, I do believe their pattern of intercession—earnestly seeking God for revival, for healing, for help and conviction—reproves us for our prayerlessness, our indifference and our ignorance of prevailing prayer.

May God help us to learn something of the power of intercessory prayer, a lesson my generation yet needs to learn. With the disciples we need to cry, "Lord, teach us to pray."

Think on This

1. Do you think that Rees Howells should be a model for us to emulate or simply one to be admired—an unusual, deeply committed person?

2. Intercessory prayer is protracted, intense prayer, something which every child of God can engage in. You pray and pray until you feel that God has heard you, then you begin to rejoice and to thank Him for what He has done. Learn more about this kind of prayer.

PRAYING WITHOUT AN AGENDA

"I tell you the truth, anyone who has faith in me will do what I have been doing. He will do even greater things than these, because I am going to the Father. And I will do whatever you ask in my name." (John 14:12-13)

Dr. Theodore F. Adams tells of a little boy who explained that he did not say his prayers every night because there were some nights he really didn't need anything. Could this possibly have been you at some time? Have there been other times in your life when you felt that you would do anything if God would only answer?

Perhaps you were in a trench facing enemy soldiers. It may have been in the narrow halls of a hospital corridor when you stood outside the room of your little child who was at the point of death. Possibly you prayed when your wife was about to leave you and you said, "God, I'll do anything, but don't let that happen!" Now the crisis is past. The smoke from the battle has cleared. Your child is well again. Your wife is by your side. God answered that prayer. But now what?

Many people miss one of the greatest blessings of life by not learning that prayer is an ongoing, open line to God's power. In writing to a group of believers at Thessalonica, Paul said, "Pray continually" (1 Thessalonians 5:17). Someone might say, "I can understand how Paul could give that kind of advice. He was either facing the Romans or the lions. He probably needed to pray quite a bit. But I have to earn a living. How can I pray all the time?" You begin to think of your busy schedule, your workload.

Keep an ear open to God so that He can give you guidance and direction every moment of the day.

Life in the morning of the twenty-first century is a far cry from the slow pace of the first century; yet Paul's advice is more contemporary than anything you will find in a current medical journal. Paul is not suggesting that you spend twenty-four hours a day on your knees before God in prayer. But he is suggesting that you constantly maintain contact with heaven. He is saying, "Keep an ear open to God so that He can give you guidance and direction every moment of the day."

Every moment of your day must count if you are to get everything done, including the things you did not get done yesterday—at the shop, in your business conferences, while you work around the house. It is a pretty crude analogy, but Paul is suggesting that prayer is something like a two-way communication system such as an airplane pilot might use. It does not mean that you are talking to God every moment, but it does mean the channel is clear so He can give you guidance beyond human ability. It is that simple.

Most of us think of prayer as just asking for something, which is only a small part of prayer. Like the little boy who prayed only when he wanted something, we often think of praying *only* when we are up against it and our backs are to the wall. But more than just asking, prayer is listening and reporting for orders. I am not

Insight

Prayer is more than a message you want to send to God. It includes listening, worship, meditation, being in the presence of the Almighty and much more.

suggesting that prayer is spiritual therapy that relieves you of all tension and fear, but I will point out that when you learn to communicate with God twenty-four hours a day, tension will lessen.

Your fears will cease to be your master because you will realize that you are not battling it alone, that success or failure does not rest on what *you* do. In the moment of stress you will hear Him remind you of His promise, "Never will I leave you; never will I forsake you" (Hebrews 13:5). Jesus said, "If you remain in me and my words remain in you, ask whatever you wish, and it will be given you" (John 15:7). The *if* makes the difference.

The Bible gives us the guidelines to eternal life. The way is through Christ, who is the difference between life and death. But God gives to each of us the power of choice—the power of accepting or rejecting, the choice of power or weakness. Prayer is the key to finding His presence and power every moment of every day.

Think on This

1. Please finish this statement: "Prayer is the key to _____."

2. On a scale of 1-10, how important is prayer with you?

ONE MAN'S PRAYER

*"The prayer of a righteous man is powerful
and effective." (James 5:16)*

Never underestimate the power of the individual, regardless of how helpless he may feel. Today, Charles Colson, the one-time aide to a U.S. President, is working among men in prison because of the prayers of an unknown prisoner in a federal penitentiary. It happened like this. Colson was involved in the Watergate affair and later became a Christian. His confession of his involvement in the scandal led him to prison, where he spent seven months. There he experienced all the frustration and turmoil that confronts men, but he also experienced the power of Jesus Christ to bring peace and harmony to men who had very little to live for. In prison, Colson started praying and studying the Bible with inmates, some of whom experienced remarkable answers to prayer that transformed their lives.

After he was released from prison, Colson went to the head of the Bureau of U.S. Prisons, requesting permission to go into the jails and work with the men, involving them in Bible studies and sharing with them the impact that a personal faith in Jesus Christ can make in a person's life. But the man who was responsible was not convinced. He decided to take it under consideration, and Colson walked out of his office feeling defeated.

Later, however, the Chief of the Bureau of Prisons happened to slip into a chapel service at the Terminal Island Prison. He came unannounced and sat in the back where it was dark. One by one the men lifted their voices in prayer—hardened criminals for whom there was little hope of rehabilitation through the traditional prison life. He saw something in these men that he knew had to be God's working.

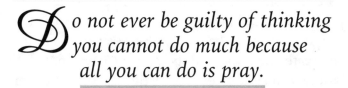

Do not ever be guilty of thinking you cannot do much because all you can do is pray.

Suddenly, a prisoner stood to his feet and began praying for this very man. He had no idea that the man for whom he was praying was in the room, but when the Chief of Prisons heard his name mentioned, he choked up. The prisoner prayed for the jailer, and it was that prayer which came from the lips of an unknown man that opened the doors of federal prisons for Chuck Colson to share Christ. It may well be that this man will never know how God used his prayers until he stands on heaven's shore, but a man who thought he could not do much accomplished through prayer what senators and congressmen could not do.

Do not ever be guilty of thinking you cannot do much because all you can do is pray. That is like saying prayer is not as important as money, influence or prestige. Quite often I hear from people who say, "All I can do is pray for you." I feel like shouting, "Don't ever say, 'All I can do is pray for you!' because that is tremendous if you will really do it."

Prayer is costly, though. It means that we are willing to set aside our personal interests, and more than that, our pride, and bend the knee in hum-

Insight

The prayers of an inmate—a convict who had become a prisoner of Jesus Christ—made a big difference to the head of the Bureau of U.S. Prisons, and he allowed Chuck Colson and others to evangelize and work in prisons.

ble submission. If prayer were based on chance or happenstance, the results might well be rather inconsequential, but because prayer is based on a relationship of a child with the Father, a great deal can be accomplished through prayer. To the Galatians Paul wrote, "Because you are sons, God sent the Spirit of his Son into our hearts, the Spirit who calls out, '*Abba,* Father' " (Galatians 4:6). Tremendous!

The tragedy of our hour is that so many individuals have never discovered how great a power is the power of prayer. In troubled marriages it can accomplish what no counselor can ever do. In times of difficulty, it not only can unlock prison doors, but also restore broken relationships and set the captive free. Remember that the prisoner who could never walk into government offices and make his influence felt could pray, and God used his humble prayer to accomplish what free, powerful men could not do. Take heart, and remember the great power of prayer.

Think on This

1. Have you ever been guilty of saying, "I'll pray for you," then promptly forgot that you made a commitment? Strive to write down things that you pray for.
2. Suggestion: When someone wants you to pray for him, make a commitment of a definite period of time, say, thirty days. Then find out what has happened. This is more effective as well in that the person for whom you are praying knows you are praying and accepts some obligation to let you know what happens.

ANSWERS TO PRAYERS
WE NEVER PRAYED

*"The men of Israel sampled their provisions
but did not inquire of the LORD." (Joshua 9:14)*

"**H**eaven is full of answers to prayers for which no one ever bothered to ask." So says the venerable Billy Graham. How often do we go plodding on, sometimes blundering, getting ourselves into situations which turn into nightmares because we never bother to stop long enough and say, "God, what do You want me to do? Is this Your will, or does it simply look pretty good to me?" Answers to prayers that were never prayed could have saved you all kinds of headaches.

Long ago Joshua and his staff could have saved themselves all kinds of heartaches had they only stopped long enough to ask God for guidance. Here's how they got themselves into trouble. After God gave them two great victories—one at Jericho and Ai—they met together and renewed their commitment to serve

God. The law was read and the people nodded their heads in agreement.

But shortly after that the Gibeonites, having heard what Joshua had done to Jericho and Ai, decided they had better sue for peace. They resorted to a ruse: They went as a delegation whose donkeys were loaded with worn-out sacks and old wineskins, cracked and mended. The men put worn and patched sandals on their feet and wore old clothes. All of the bread of their food supply was dry and moldy. "We have come from a distant country, make a treaty with us," they said.

Even Joshua was fooled as they told him how the bread that was now dry and moldy had been soft and fresh when they started their trip. Yes, of course they lied. But they were convincing. And Joshua signed a treaty with them, agreeing to conditions whereby they would be servants to the Israelites but never would be killed.

It's OK to acknowledge that you don't know what to do and to ask God for wisdom and direction.

The key to their failure is summed up in a few words which Joshua himself later wrote, "The men of Israel sampled their provisions but did not inquire of the LORD" (Joshua 9:14). They sniffed the moldy bread, and ran their fingers through the worn and ragged garments, and bought into their lies which they told with consummate skill.

Do you realize that the overconfidence which led to Joshua's failure is still with us today? Nobody is so smart, so savvy, so discerning that he can't be deceived by the enemies in life, to say nothing of the devil who is a master of deception. That's why bringing God into your negotiations, asking Him for direction and guidance, is so important.

God's answers to prayers you should have prayed but didn't could keep you from making terrible mistakes: entering into a marriage which turns into a nightmare, or signing on the dotted line, committing yourself to something you will later regret.

Insight

Overconfidence often prods us into acting on our own. If we only took time to ask God for wisdom, He would give us spiritual insights which would save us from failure.

James, the half-brother of Jesus, gave us a powerful promise when he wrote, "If any of you lacks wisdom, he should ask God, who gives generously to all without finding fault, and it will be given to him" (James 1:5). It's OK to acknowledge that you don't know what to do and to ask God for wisdom and direction.

Someone wisely said, "He who knows not and *knows* that he knows not is a wise man, but he who knows not and knows *not* that he knows not is a fool."

Are you in need of an answer to a prayer that you have not yet prayed? God won't thump you over the head to get your attention, but He will respond to your simple cry of, "Lord, I need Your help. What should I do? What is Your will in this whole matter?"

If you are married, make it a practice to join hands and hearts with your husband or wife and pray together before you make any major decisions. If you are single, start each day asking God to guide and direct you. He will! Those answers to prayer we never pray are there, as Billy Graham suggested, ready to save us from our own mistakes and presumption.

Think on This

1. Most of the mistakes in life involving judgment are made when we act without consulting God and/or spiritual men and women who might see potential dangers we overlooked in haste. In your own life, what might have been avoided had you sought for God's will as opposed to blindly moving ahead?

2. What causes us to hesitate to say, "God, I really need Your help!"? Do you sometimes see yourself as your greatest enemy?

$\mathcal{H}$OW MANY TIMES MUST YOU ASK?

"Father, I thank you that you have heard me.
I knew that you always hear me, but I said this
for the benefit of the people standing here, that
they may believe that you sent me." (John 11:41-42)

$\mathcal{H}$ow many times must you pray the same prayer and ask God to do the same thing before He hears you? Once, twice, or day after day until you get what you are asking for? Tough question, right? There are times when something bothers you and you pray about it. Nothing seems to happen so you pray again and again. Or may you give up entirely, thinking you don't know the right words; or you think, *This may work for others but not for me!*

Jesus, anticipating that this would be one of the issues of concern for us, told a story about a widow who lived in a certain town where there was a judge who cared neither for God nor for people. Luke, the physician, records it in the passage found in Luke 18.

Someone took advantage of this widow Jesus told us about, so she went to a judge and asked for justice. For some time he was indifferent and refused to deal with the situation. Day after day, the woman came back with the same request. Finally the judge relented. He said, "Even though I don't fear God or care about men, yet because this widow keeps bothering me, I will see that she gets justice, so that she won't eventually wear me out with her coming!" (Luke 18:4-5).

Jesus prefaced the story saying that the disciples "should always pray and not give up" (18:1). You may say, "OK, should we, like the widow, keep on knocking on heaven's door until we get an answer?"

There are times when you need to prevail in prayer, asking God to do what you feel is His will.

First, let me point out a couple of things you need to know. The picture of the judge who is indifferent and guilty of catering to the rich and famous isn't a true picture of our Heavenly Father, who is no respecter of persons. Money and prestige don't open the door to the throne room of heaven. Furthermore, I think it can fairly be said that God is on the side of the little widow, the insignificant person who is denied justice and fairness in life today. Payer is not about trying with great difficulty to get justice out of a corrupt system.

The New Testament says clearly that prayer is based on the relationship of a child with the father. Make a note of Galatians 4, which tells us that we are adopted by our Heavenly Father and become His children through faith in His Son, Jesus Christ.

Now, let's go back to that original question, "How many times must you ask God to do something before you know He has heard you?" Let me ask you a second question: "When you were a child, how many times did you have to ask your father for something before he responded to you?" Once you got his attention, he answered you, right? He always gave you what you wanted, right? No, sometimes he loved you too much to give you what you asked for.

Insight

Often God's timetable is different from ours. Patience is learning to trust God, believing that He has heard our plea, when we still have nothing to show for it.

There are times when you need to prevail in prayer, asking God to do what you feel is His will. You sense that you have connected with heaven, but you don't yet have the answer. From that point on, you don't need to keep on asking the same thing, but begin to thank Him in advance for His answer and wait patiently for Him to do what you have asked. As Jesus put it, "Your Father knows what you need before you ask him" (Matthew 6:8). When you know He's heard, you eventually get a clear answer. It really happens.

Think on This

1. How would you answer someone who asked, "How many times should I pray for something?"
2. What's the difference between "vain repetition," which Jesus condemned, and praying always without giving up? Is it vain repetition when your child says, "Mommy, I love you"?

ᏉOING ONE-ON-ONE WITH GOD IN TRUSTING HIM

"But my God shall supply all your need according to his riches in glory by Christ Jesus." (Philippians 4:19, KJV)

"ᏉIVE us this day our daily bread," were the words of Jesus when His disciples came to Him with the request, "Lord, teach us to pray." Nothing is more basic than food, and when you lack it, and you go one-on-one with God, asking Him to meet that need, and He does it in such a way that you know it was He who did it, your faith grows. You know that God answered your prayer.

Guy and Audrey Duffield had that experience the year after God gave them a baby girl, who some twenty-one years later became my wife. Here's how Pop (as I knew him) described it:

In the year 1935, Mrs. Duffield and I were pastoring a small church. It was our first church after we had been married. After several years there we felt that our ministry in that place was finished and so we talked with the district supervisor about the possibility of a move. He offered us another pastorate. The monthly reports from this church showed that it had a considerably larger membership than the one which we had been pastoring. I am not going to say that this did not influence our agreeing to go there; however, upon our arrival we discovered this larger membership was only on the monthly reports. They were certainly not in the church pews. In fact, the actual membership was much smaller than the church we had left.

Just to think that we had a God who loved us enough to even keep track of the number of potatoes in our sack!

To our surprise we found that our weekly salary was to be $10. Those were the Great Depression days. Only one man in the church had steady work. We were, of course, considerably taken aback by these circumstances, and we wondered how we were going to make out.

We had only been there a few days when a farmer backed his little white pickup truck into our yard and unloaded a 100-pound sack of potatoes into our shed. And Mr. Smith said, "When these are gone, let me know and I'll bring you another sack." We thanked him from grateful hearts and bade him good-bye.

One hundred pounds of potatoes! We felt like millionaires. We were rich. You can do so many different things with potatoes. You can boil them, bake them, fry them, hash-brown them, scallop them, stuff them, au gratin them, etc. We really enjoyed those potatoes.

But after some weeks had gone by I noticed that the potatoes in the sack were going down and down. And then I remembered what Brother Smith had said: "When these are gone, give me a call and I'll bring you another sack."

I do not know whether it was pride or stubbornness, but I could no more have called Brother Smith and said, "Brother Smith, we need some more potatoes," than I could have jumped off a cliff. But I did get down on my knees and pray, "Lord, will You tell Brother Smith that we need some more potatoes?"

Insight

If your Heavenly Father can keep track of the number of hairs on your head, keeping track of the small potatoes is no big problem for Him.

Do you know, it was less than two weeks later that the little white pickup truck stopped at our back door and Brother Smith unloaded another 100-pound sack of potatoes for our use and put it down by the other sack. And when I looked in the first sack there were exactly two potatoes left.

Did we get blessed! Just to think that we had a God who loved us enough to even keep track of the number of potatoes in our sack! That simple experience has given me faith to believe God, in the years that followed, to raise tens of thousands of dollars for the work of the Lord.

Dr. Duffield always looked back at that incident as a defining event in his life as he learned that going one-on-one with God produces rich results. Paul was right when he said, "But my God shall supply all your need according to his riches in glory by Christ Jesus" (Philippians 4:19, KJV).

Think on This

If God can feed the sparrow, can He not make note of the small, seemingly inconsequential needs in your life? Remember the small answer. It will help you trust Him for the greater need in the future.

GOING ONE-ON-ONE WITH GOD IN PRAYER

"Father, if you are willing, take this cup from me; yet not my will, but yours be done." (Luke 22:42)

Of all the sites in Israel which are significant, none touches my emotions more than visiting the Garden of Gethsemane on the gentle slopes of the Mount of Olives, across from the walled city where the golden dome of the Mosque of Omar glistens in the sun and glows in the moonlight.

What is so touching about Gethsemane? Well, for one thing, we are relatively certain that here was where Jesus, burdened with the tremendous load of what was happening, poured out His anguish before God. The gnarled olive trees in the garden are old—very old. Botanists believe that either they grew from tender shoots of trees which were there at the time of Jesus' sojourn on earth or else they were already growing as actual trees.

The word *Gethsemane* means "olive press," and today you still see the great mill stones that pressed the olives, producing the oil used for cooking, for lamps and for healing. As the cross loomed before Him, Jesus took the disciples and went to Gethsemane, where He went one-on-one with the Father. Luke tells us that a short distance from the disciples, Jesus knelt down and prayed, "Father, if you are willing, take this cup from me; yet not my will, but yours be done" (Luke 22:42).

There was no crowd, not even the twelve who had fallen asleep—only Jesus, who knelt and prayed. A shroud of loneliness covered the spot, a feeling more than a few have experienced at the point of absolute desperation, kneeling in humility before God and pouring out their anguish in fervent prayer, sealed with burning tears. Nothing can be deeper, more serious or meaningful.

> *Never be afraid to go one-on-one with God in the hour of need, for only then will you discover His grace.*

In Jesus' example and prayer, I see several guidelines which form a pattern when we face the Gethsemane of our lives. *First, Jesus prayed to the Father.* This speaks of a relationship. He knew He was the Son of God. Nothing is more fundamental when it comes to answered prayer than knowing you have become a son of God through faith in Jesus Christ, adopted into the great family of

God. It is because you are a son that God hears your prayer.

Then Jesus prayed personally. It was something He had to do, and it is something that you must do as you too go one-on-one with God. *Jesus also prayed persistently.* Matthew tells us that three times Jesus poured out His soul in deep, fervent prayer. This was God's Son. *Doesn't God hear my prayer the first time I pray?* Yes, but there are times when we must prevail in prayer, holding to the promises of God, bringing our thoughts to focus on what we are asking God to do.

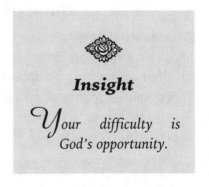

Insight

Your difficulty is God's opportunity.

Jesus also prayed according to the will of God. The traditional text says Jesus prayed, saying, "Father, if thou be willing, remove this cup from me: nevertheless not my will, but thine, be done" (Luke 22:42, KJV). The highest form of faith is praying "nevertheless" as you yield to the will of the Father, trusting Him for His grace and strength to do what He wants. It always leaves open the door for God to answer your prayer differently from how you think He should.

And what happened? Did God deliver Him so that He would not have to drink of the cup? No, God sent an angel who strengthened Him as He prayed even more earnestly.

Frankly, God does not always deliver you from the evil or the need that drives you to go one-on-one with Him, but He does give you the strength and the grace to endure and to do so joyfully.

Never, never be afraid to go one-on-one with God in the hour of need, for only then will you discover His grace.

Think on This

1. Does the fact that Jesus prayed three times specifically for the same thing speak to your heart?
2. What about the disciples? Can you relate to their problem—weariness and sleepiness? What did they miss by sleeping through this encounter that Christ had with the Father?

$\mathcal{G}$OING ONE-ON-ONE WITH GOD IN FAITH

*"Therefore I tell you, whatever you ask for
in prayer, believe that you have received it,
and it will be yours." (Mark 11:24)*

$\mathcal{S}$hortly after Dallas Seminary was founded in 1924, the world began slipping into a financial crisis which became known as the Great Depression. Money was scarce, and it became evident that if God didn't do something big, and soon, the creditors of the fledgling school were going to foreclose and take the property. And what do you do when there is a financial need? Some would write letters of financial appeal. Some would call their donors and hit the panic button. But not the leadership of this school, which placed strong emphasis on the authority of the Word. The leaders prayed. Nothing more? No, but they didn't just pray. They *really* prayed.

Gathering in the office of the president, Dr. Lewis Sperry Chafer, they asked God to undertake. Present in that prayer meeting was a man who had memorized most of the New Testament while he was still a teenager—Harry Ironside, a kind of no-nonsense, get-straight-to-the-point sort of person. His prayers were no different. "Lord," he began, pausing somewhat like a locomotive when it emits the first great whoosh of steam, ready to start moving in great momentum. Continuing, he said, "we know that the cattle on a thousand hills are Thine. Please sell some of them and send the money."

They were still praying when a lanky cowboy, weathered from the outdoors, with callused hands and wearing cowboy boots, walked into the business office of the school and announced, "I just sold two carloads of cattle. . . . I've been trying to make a business deal but it fell through, and I feel compelled to give the money to the seminary. I don't know if you need it or not, but here is the check!"

The young woman, knowing that a prayer meeting was going on at that very moment in the office of the president, took the check and gently knocked on the door where the group prayed. Dr. Chafer took the check and immediately noticed that the amount of the check was exactly the amount which they needed—neither more nor less. "Harry," he said, "God sold the cattle!"[1]

Long ago the psalmist recorded the words of the Creator, who said, "For all the animals of field and forest are mine! The cattle on a thousand hills! And all the birds upon the mountains!" (Psalm 50:10-11, Living Bible). If God owns the cattle on a thousand hills, how do we, like the men who prayed in the office of Dr. Chafer, get God to send a few our way?

Five guidelines—all from Scripture—answer that question.

Guideline #1: Pray specifically

Take time to go back to Matthew 6 and study the passage we call The Lord's Prayer. Then study the prayers of Jesus and what He asked for. He prayed for specifics. If you need the hind-quarter of beef, then ask the Lord specifically for that. If you need $50,000, ask God for that specific amount.

Guideline #2: Pray persistently

Even Jesus in Gethsemane prayed the same thing three times. When you have prayed

Insight

One of the direct results of bringing your needs to Him is the certainty that He—not luck or chance or fate—answered and provided for your needs.

and prayed and the Spirit of God finally witnesses to your heart that God has heard you, thank Him in advance for your answer.

Guideline #3: Pray biblically

Gently reminding God of His many promises in the Word establishes a connection between you and God's goodness.

Guideline #4: Pray in faith

James says anyone who doubts is like a wave of the sea, driven and tossed by the wind. That person gets nothing from the Father. (See James 1:6.)

Guideline #5: Pray earnestly

James says, "The down-to-business prayer of a man who has been justified brings great gain" (James 5:16, personal translation).

A closing thought: When you ask God for one of the cattle on the hills, better fire up the barbecue or start looking for a buyer.

Think on This

1. Take the five guidelines which are found in today's selection and use them as a model when you pray.
2. Harry Ironside—the man who prayed that God would sell some of the cattle on the hills—has been an inspiration to many, myself included. It was his knowledge of the Word which gave him that confidence. The more you know of the Word, the greater will be your confidence in prayer (see Romans 10:17).

1   James Hewett, *Illustrations Unlimited* (Wheaton, IL: Tyndale House, 1988), p. 148. Used by permission of Tyndale House Publishers. All rights reserved.

$\mathcal{W}$HEN GOD'S ANSWER DOESN'T MATCH YOUR REQUEST

· " 'For my thoughts are not your thoughts,
neither are your ways my ways,'
declares the LORD." (Isaiah 55:8)

$\mathcal{H}$ave you ever prayed, yet it seemed your prayers were bouncing off the ceiling? You cried from your heart, but it seemed that God did not hear you. Perhaps you were like the little boy who prayed that his dog would not die, and when it did, he responded, "Well, God must be dead because He sure didn't answer my prayer." Though you may not have expressed yourself so bluntly, in the depths of your heart you may have questioned the outcome. You may well have wondered why God did not intervene on your behalf.

The wife of Dr. Joseph Parker, pastor of the great City Temple in London for many years, contracted a serious illness and for many weeks endured intense suffering.

Hours on end Joseph Parker waited by the bed, hoping, trusting and praying that God would spare her the suffering, yet she lingered on and on. In a moment of weakness Parker was gripped with doubts of God's existence. Dr. Parker said that if he had a dog that had suffered like his wife, he would have killed it to put it out of its misery.

When suffering or tragedy strikes, it is not unusual to be driven to the depths of despair. In the hour of crisis we first blame God and think that He has failed, because God has not done what we thought should have been done. This is not any real indication that God has failed or that He has ceased to love us. Could it be that God will let situations happen so that we will find that beyond our deepest grief is the love of God to comfort and sustain?

> *Let God do for you what you cannot do for yourself, and find peace for your troubled heart.*

It is perfectly normal for your heart to cry out, "Why?" "Why did it have to happen to *me*?" You feel isolated and alone. In all probability you feel utterly inadequate to cope with the situation. For the first time in your life you feel that you are helpless. But what appears to be tragedy can become a victory in a deep way. When you have reached the end of your resources, you acknowledge the fact that you cannot go on without sustaining strength. If all of us had every prayer answered, we would never learn the depths of God's comforting presence, for otherwise we would be self-sufficient and would really have no need of God. But facing the despair of the midnight hour, you are forced to seek the strength of God as you would never have done if He had answered your desire when you first prayed.

In the book of Isaiah we are told that God's ways are above our ways, and His thoughts are above our thoughts (see Isaiah 55:8). We usually picture God as someone about like ourselves, different in the sense that He is above time and space, but basically we think of God much in terms of human existence. Actually, God tran-

Insight

When we "lean not to our own understanding" as Proverbs 3:5-6 tells us to do, we begin to trust God's heart when we cannot see His hand.

scends the loftiest thought you will ever have, yet His presence goes deeper than the deepest sorrow you ever face. Since God is above the laws of time and space, He sees the end from the beginning. You can see only the immediate present.

Suppose that you saw a tiny ant crawling on an eight-foot piece of lumber. Now the ant could see only the immediate present. In fact, if you placed your hand in front of him, he could see absolutely nothing ahead. You, however, could see both the beginning and the ending of that eight-foot board which served as the path the ant would travel. God views our lives much in the same perspective. He allows the catastrophes to serve as fire that refines the dross and produces the pure gold. He sees the silver lining to the darkest cloud of doom. God's Word says that He is a stronghold in the day of trouble. It tells us that He is near those of a broken heart.

After you have exhausted your resources, let hope in the goodness of God lift you from the sadness of your despair. In the darkest hour, Christ wishes to whisper, "Peace, be still," and bring rest to your troubled heart. He will give you a settled tranquillity that goes deeper than the turbulent present. Jesus said, "All that the Father gives me will come to me, and whoever comes to me I will never drive away" (John 6:37). In all probability you have tried everything else. Let God do for you what you cannot do for yourself, and find peace for your troubled heart.

Think on This

1. Look back on a situation you faced, one which you could not understand at the time it happened. Now, later, do you see any good which has come from it?
2. Does the attitude of Job—"though He slay me, yet will I hope in Him" (Job 13:15)—come to bear on some difficult situations, ones we don't understand?
3. Tell God in no uncertain terms how you feel. It's OK. He already knows.

$\mathcal{W}$HEN GOD SAYS, "MY GRACE IS ENOUGH!"

"Three times I pleaded with the Lord to take it away from me. But he said to me, 'My grace is sufficient for you, for my power is made perfect in weakness.' " (2 Corinthians 12:8-9)

$\mathcal{P}$aul's letter to the Corinthians, known as Second Corinthians in the New Testament, is called "the heart of Paul" because in this letter Paul opens his heart and shares something of the frustration and turmoil he endured. In this letter he tells how his life was made miserable by an affliction—probably a physical handicap—which he described as a "thorn in the flesh," a messenger from Satan that buffeted his life.

No one knows for certain what that affliction was. Migraine headaches, eye trouble, malaria, even epilepsy have all been suggested. Dr. David Van Reken, a medical doctor, believes that Paul's thorn was an ophthalmic condition producing near blindness, caused, perhaps, by the intensely bright light which arrested Paul on the road to Damascus.

Writing to the Galatians, Paul commented, "See what large letters I use as I write to you"—perhaps because he was nearly blind. Earlier he had written, "You would have torn out your eyes and given them to me" had that been possible (see Galatians 6:11 and 4:15).

Had Paul told us exactly what his thorn was, scores of us, perhaps you included, would have been deprived of a great truth because we would reason, "My thorn is different from Paul's." But this way all of us can identify with that thorn in the flesh which Paul prayed about three times, specifically asking God to remove it. But God chose not to give Paul his request; instead He gave him something greater to teach him something more valuable—that His grace can meet us at the point of our deepest need.

Often, God has something even greater for us—the ongoing lesson that His grace is sufficient to help us learn to live with our "thorn in the flesh."

True, there are times when God spectacularly removes the thorn—the cancer goes into remission and disappears, the tiny holes in the heart of the baby that should have died gradually mend, the lame walk and the blind see. Yet often God has something even greater for us—the ongoing lesson that His grace is sufficient to help us learn to live with our "thorn in the flesh."

Dr. Ralph Keiper had to live with a "thorn in the flesh." In his youth, medication that was much too strong robbed him of most of his sight, yet that did not stop him from a life of service for his Lord. One day a friend, bothered with poor vision herself, asked Keiper if it was annoying to him, struggling with only twenty percent of his vision. Keiper, a rotund little man barely five feet tall, replied, "Oh, no, God wants me to see through His eyes."

God's answer to Paul was simple: "My grace is sufficient for you"—the only place in Scripture where God directly speaks of His grace. The Greek word for sufficient speaks of unfailing strength. And the phrase that follows, "My power is made perfect in weakness" (2 Corinthians 12:9), bears the force of a definite and powerful answer.

Insight

At times you cannot see the grand design and purpose of God; thus, when your requests are denied, the highest form of faith is to trust Him and thus learn that His grace is sufficient.

At times God's removing the thorn—which He can and sometimes does—almost pales in comparison with His grace which meets you day by day, especially those of you who wrestle with your thorn on an ongoing basis.

Paul then told us that he gloried, he actually took pleasure, in his weakness, for he had learned that God actually delights to show how strong He is when we realize how weak we are.

It is not the strong person—the one who has need of nothing, or the self-sufficient, independent person who needs no one's help (including God's)—but the individual who understands how weak he is who is in a position to receive the abundant help which God describes as His grace.

Think on This

1. How have you seen God's grace manifested in your personal life when things you have asked God to do didn't come together? Are you far enough removed from the disappointment to taste of His sufficiency and grace?
2. Would your life be poorer spiritually if God answered all your prayers just as you prayed them?

When the Grass Is Growing on Your Path

"Always keep on praying."
(1 Thessalonians 5:17, Living Bible)

Christian brother who lives in Africa tells about the men and women in his village who felt a need to have a place of prayer where they could escape from the rest of the tribe and find a quiet, peaceful place of solitude. Since they lived in a populous village, finding such a place became a challenge. But they began going out into the forest at the break of day to read their Bibles and pray. The African brother telling the story said that now, if one becomes unfaithful and neglects taking time for prayer, the other believers will soon notice and reprimand him by saying, "Brother, the grass is beginning to grow on your path."

Whether you live in Africa or in Tokyo or Manila, it is not easy to find time each day for prayer and Bible study.

Yet nothing is more important to your spiritual development than taking time for prayer. S.D. Gordon wrote this about the importance of prayer:

> The greatest thing anyone can do for God and man is to pray. It is not the only thing; but it is the chief thing. The great people of the earth today are the people who pray. I do not mean those who talk about prayer; not those who say they believe in prayer; nor yet those who can explain about prayer; but I mean those people who take time to pray.

As our African friends put it, "Is there grass growing on the path to your prayer closet?" In other words, do you find time in a busy schedule to put the practice of prayer into operation? You may be one of those who is convinced that prayer is important, but you do not get around to bending the knee. Priorities have to determine the use of our time, because when it comes to our time, we all have exactly the same amount.

You can just let the words flow out of your heart in conversation with God.

I know a very successful surgeon who spends the first hour of his day, regardless of whether it is 4 a.m. or 7 a.m., in prayer and study. This man does not just find time, he takes it. I know businessmen who meet with their staff for prayer before they open their doors. Does it work? They believe it is the best thing they ever do to insure a smooth working relationship in the office.

Prayer is the oil that makes the machinery run smoothly. But it is more than this. To pray, you do not have to recite words out of a prayer book or go through a ritual; you can just let the words flow out of your heart in conversation with God.

One of the greatest misconceptions of our day is that prayer is reserved for only the professionals and those about to face a bullet in a foxhole. Don't you believe it! Theologians may not fully understand it, but the least significant child of God can put it into practice. You can pray about every-thing—your personal needs, your spouse, your children, your neighborhood, your world. You can pray about specific needs of your family and friends—physical, emo-tional and spiritual

Insight

The amount of time you spend in prayer—not what you say you believe about prayer—really indicates how strongly you believe its power.

needs too. Pray for your government; for officials; for fellow Christians; even pray for your enemies, asking God to touch their lives; you can pray about anything, anytime. "You may ask me for anything in my name, and I will do it" Jesus told His disciples (John 14:14).

I just picked up a new edition of *The Merriam-Webster Dictionary*, and among the definitions of prayer is this: "a slight chance." Prayer is no chance; no happenstance of fate. It is the result of a relationship established through Jesus Christ which lets you as God's child come into His presence and share your deepest needs with your Heavenly Father. It is still the greatest power in all the world, and there is nothing that takes its place. You can prove that fact for yourself.

Think on This

1. Take a notebook and record specific prayer requests.
2. As you pray, ponder what God would have you do about situations.

ᑭRAYING WITHOUT THE AMEN

"Pray without ceasing." (1 Thessalonians 5:17, KJV)

"𝓘 was blessed with a wonderful mother," says David Moore, "[who] taught me how to pray for all things, great and small, and then to trust Him to answer in the way that was best for me."

David says that as a boy he noticed that when his mother prayed, she never said, "Amen," at the end of her prayers. When he went to church and the pastor prayed, he always finished with a flourish and a hearty, "Amen." That, of course, was the sign that the prayer was ended and it was time to head for the door. When others prayed, they always signed off with an "Amen," as a kind of spiritual radio station break signaling the conclusion of the whole matter. But not *his* mother, and it bothered David.

One day he asked her, "Mother, why don't you ever say 'Amen'?"

And she answered, "I'm not through praying. 'Amen' denotes a conclusion to a prayer, and I'm not through yet. I am just pausing for a while." She explained, "Jesus knows that I have many duties to perform and He doesn't mind waiting for a few minutes before we continue our conversation."[1]

Is that scriptural or what? When Paul wrote to the Thessalonians he told them to "pray without ceasing" (1 Thessalonians 5:17, KJV). Another translation puts it, "Pray continually," and a third renders the text, "Always keep on praying" (Living Bible). Obviously Paul couldn't have meant that we should pray every waking moment. Even those who have entered cloisters and dedicated their lives to pray will tell you that it is impossible to focus on prayer every moment. Even the most dedicated will tell you that their minds wander, and their thoughts drift far astray.

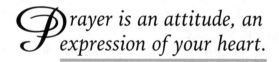

Prayer is an attitude, an expression of your heart.

What this godly woman practiced is exactly what Paul had in mind. Live day by day, hour by hour and minute by minute so that you are in touch with the Lord. Prayer is an attitude, an expression of your heart which finds expression in words. But it goes far beyond the composed verbal expressions which we think of as prayers.

After spending most of her life alone in Africa, a Scottish woman returned to her native Scotland. Mary

Slessor was admired for her work, but friends began to talk among themselves. "Have you noticed," said one, "that she mumbles to herself almost all of the time?" It seemed obvious to them that the loneliness and isolation had affected her mind. With the true loyalty of a friend who tells you about your social flaws, someone pointed out the fact that people were talking about her apparent conversation.

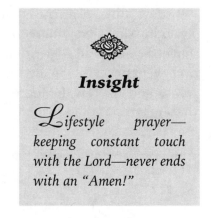

Insight

Lifestyle prayer—keeping constant touch with the Lord—never ends with an "Amen!"

Immediately Mary Slessor set them straight. "Yes," she replied, "I know what I am doing. I'm talking to Jesus." She explained that in everything she prayed and vented her feelings to the Lord.

There's a good chance that your employer might wonder whether both of your oars reach the water if you prayed audibly all of the time; but you can make it a practice, as did David Moore's mother, never to say "Amen"; never, in reality, to say, "OK, God, that's it for now. I'll be in touch with You the next time I have a need."

Prayer is conversation between you and your Heavenly Father. It's a dialogue that should never end. Though you may never have noticed this fact in the Gospels, it's interesting to observe that the prayers of Jesus were very short in public, very long in private. His conversation with His Heavenly Father ended only when He cried, "Into thy hands I commend my spirit" (Luke 23:46, KJV), and then God glorified Him as His Son and received Him into His presence.

May God forgive us for the Amens we have used to conclude our praying. Let's keep the dialogue going.

Think on This

By now you have learned that prayer is more than simply addressing God with requests. Worship, confession, conversation, praise, petition and just talking about whatever concerns you are involved. Keep the dialogue going, and as David Moore's mother did, never say "Amen."

---

1   Used by permission of David Moore.

ＯF YOU COULD ASK ONE QUESTION . . .

*"Consider therefore the kindness and sternness
of God: sternness to those who fell,
but kindness to you, provided that you continue
in his kindness." (Romans 11:22)*

Ｉf you had an opportunity to ask God just one question, what would it be? Would you ask how old
the universe really is—a question that would put to rest
once and for all the debate about the age of the Earth? Or
would you ask a theological question—say, about free will
versus the sovereign will of God?

Some would ask such questions, but I suspect your
question would be something more like one of these:
"God, why can't I have a baby which I desperately want
when other women abort children they don't want?" Or,
"God, why did my dear mother have to suffer so much
with cancer?"

The same week we said "good-bye for now" to my
father-in-law, Guy Duffield, who was almost eighty-

nine years of age, a young friend, twenty-four, having been married for just four weeks, was murdered by a man he was trying to help. Joel England had saved money and bought a little house, purposely renting it to an underprivileged ethnic family, striving to live out the love of Christ and in his way do something to bring about racial reconciliation.

As the result of a bizarre set of circumstances, much too complex to describe here, he was murdered. *Why, God?* Why does a young man who had recently graduated from Moody Bible Institute and married his sweetheart, preparing for a life of Christian service, have his life tragically cut short?

> *Ours is a sinful, broken world, and the consequences of this disharmony touch the lives of both the just and the unjust, the good and the evil, the young as well as the old.*

While good may come of evil, there are some questions in life which will never be answered this side of eternity. So what do you do? Grow angry and blame God for the sinful reaction of a man out of control? Or do you some way, somehow, find the grace of God to pick up the pieces and go on, realizing that even if God revealed the answer to the "Why?" you still couldn't understand?

When we are confronted with evil, no matter how it comes, we are shocked and reminded that ours is a sinful, broken world, and the consequences of this dishar-mony touch the lives of both the just and the unjust, the good and the evil, the young as well as the old.

Long ago David cried out, "From the end of the earth will I cry unto thee, when my heart is overwhelmed: lead me to the rock that is higher than I" (Psalm 61:2, KJV).

When your heart cries out, "Why?" strive to remember three simple guidelines:

Remember that God's nature is loving and kind—not harsh and capricious. Kindness is often misjudged as weakness. "Consider therefore the kindness and sternness of God," says Paul, adding, "sternness to those who fell, but kindness

Insight

One of the great blessings of a believer's relationship with his Heavenly Father is that, just as a child can pour out his heart to his natural father, so we can release the torrent of words which flow from the depths of our souls with the understanding that God will sift our thoughts and understand the frailties caused by the flesh.

to you, provided that you continue in his kindness" (Romans 11:22). God has His payday; someday He will right the wrongs and even the score with evildoers.

You must also remember that *God is sovereign.* Both Isaiah and Jeremiah of old struggled with the very issue and concluded: "Yet, O LORD, you are our Father. We are the clay, you are the potter; we are all the work of your hand" (Isaiah 64:8).

Finally, strive to remember that *God cares what happens to His children*. Nothing escapes His sight. Your tears and cries are never ignored. When darkness seems to surround your life, realize God too experienced this as His Son faced death at Calvary. As you can, try to remember God has been there and is now where you are. And someday you will have an answer to that question— "Why?"

Think on This

1. If you were to ask God just one question, what would it be?
2. When we arrive in heaven and sit at the feet of Jesus, do you think that knowing the answer to our cry of "Why?" will be as important as it is now?
3. Should God tell you the answer to your why, would that satisfy as much as knowing He loves you and is completely in control of your life?

Harold Sala is the founder and president of Guidelines International, a media organization reaching into more than 110 countries. A Bible teacher, radio speaker, author and world traveler, Dr. Sala holds a Ph.D. from Bob Jones University, with additional studies at other seminaries. He and his wife Darlene have three adult children and six grandchildren. They live in Mission Veijo, California.

Also by Harold Sala:

Joyfully Single in a Couples' World